THE BAYMAN

A Life on Barnegat Bay

by Merce Ridgway

Down The Shore Publishing

Recipe selections from *Chicken Foot Soup,* compiled and edited by
Arlene Martin Ridgway ©1980 Rutgers University Press. Used by permission.

For information, address:
Down The Shore Publishing Corp.
P.O. Box 100, West Creek, NJ 08092

www.down-the-shore.com

The words "Down The Shore" and the Down The Shore Publishing logo
are a registered U.S. Trademark.

Printed in the United States of America.
3 4 5 6 7 8 9 10

Book and cover design by Leslee Ganss

Library of Congress Cataloging-in-Publication Data
Ridgway, Merce.
The bayman : a life on Barnegat Bay / by Merce Ridgway.
p. cm
Includes bibliographical references and index.
ISBN 0-945582-62-5 (hc.)
1. Barnegat Bay Region (N.J.)– Social life and customs.
2. Barnegat Bay Region (N.J.) Biography. 3. Ridgway, Merce.
4. Fishers–New Jersey–Barnegat Bay Region Biography. 5. Barnegat
Bay (N.J.)–Environmental conditions.   I. Title.
F142.02R53   2000
974.9'48–dc21   99-33064

CIP

ISBN 1-59322-019-7 (trade paper)
ISBN-13 978-1-59322-019-8

*This book is dedicated to my
dear wife Arlene — who
made it happen.*

CONTENTS

Foreword

Merce Ridgway, whom I have known for twenty-five years, is a man I have always respected. I first met Merce in the 1970s while I was conducting folklore research in the coastal pines of southern New Jersey. I spent time learning about the community of musicians in the area of Waretown and Forked River in Ocean County, where Merce was one of the leading figures. I knew him first in his role as musician — singer, songwriter, guitarist, and band leader.

I celebrated Merce in my published research, and I presented his musical performances at the New Jersey Folk Festival in New Brunswick and at other concert venues throughout the state. Of course, he was a skillful musician and a gifted songwriter. But what fascinated me most was that he was an exemplar of tradition. His father, Merce Ridgway, Sr., also a singer-songwriter, had been one of the original Pinehawkers who were selected by the folklorist Dorothea Dix Lawrence to represent New Jersey at the 1941 National Folk Festival at Constitution Hall in Washington, D.C.

So it was Merce's music and his ties to tradition that first brought us together. However, as I spent more time with him, I realized that Merce's real life was that of a bayman, which is the focus of this book. In this remarkable and highly readable memoir, Merce tells us of growing up near Barnegat Bay where he spent time fishing, crabbing, and clamming. These passages come alive with a vivid sense of imagery — the smell of fresh paint on duck decoys, the sounds of a sawmill cutting cedar logs, or the sweet taste of tender muskrat meat.

After a tour of duty in the Marine Corps, Merce returned to the Barnegat Bay area, got married, and raised a family. It's a story filled with love and humor and occasional sadness. After spending years on the water, Merce is able to tell us how to catch a clam, how to process scallops, and how to avoid being pinched by a crab. We cannot help but admire Merce for his keen observation of nature, his knowledge of the construction and maintenance of fishing equipment, not to mention his values of individualism and self-sufficiency.

What makes the story poignant is that, in the end, Merce was unable to continue as a bayman in New Jersey. Merce, like many others, finally gave up his traditional way of life. What was the problem? Alas, there was no one answer. Instead, there were many issues, including overpopulation, pollution, reduced stocks of shellfish, high taxes, and meddlesome bureaucrats. Barnegat Bay, Merce tells us, is not what it once was — a reliable source of income and food. That's the sad part, but at least we now have this wonderful book which gives us an honest portrait of a vanishing way of life.

— ANGUS KRESS GILLESPIE
Associate Professor of American Studies, Rutgers University
New Brunswick, New Jersey

The original Pinehawkers — (left to right) Bill Britton, Merce Ridgway, Sr. and Walt Britton — with folklorist Dorothea Dix Lawrence at a radio session in New York City.

Preface

In my youth, the boats were of wood and the men were of iron.

Merce Ridgway

The words of earlier writers transport us to the times and the lives they lived. Often, we wish they had told us more. Sometimes the details that would interest us most are elusive, lost between the lines; so commonplace they simply weren't set down to paper.

Because change came slowly in earlier times, the writer may have seen no need to discuss everyday details which it seemed to him would never fade. And so history has many blank pages that will never be filled.

Our own lives, those of us who are older, have seen many changes. In my youth the boats were of wood and the men were of iron. If we look for them today, we find them mostly in memory.

By leaving a record, I hope to shed a small light on a culture that has all but disappeared in the span of one lifetime. Maybe those who come later will find less of a mystery and as readers, live again the life of a bayman on Barnegat Bay.

I had a dream a short while back. I was running along in my garvey close to the west bank, up by Wrangle Point. It was a bright, sunny, spring-like day, although a stiff and cold west wind blew off the meadows. I spied my father's boat, anchored bow to the wind. He was sitting in the sun out of the weather, behind his shelter cabin. He was eating his lunch. I brought my boat around and tied it to his while he watched. I picked up my Thermos and lunch pail as I prepared to join him.

He grinned, and waving his sandwich, half wrapped in waxed paper, said, "You finally decided to come see me again!"

I was pleased and happy, and so was he. I was enjoying the pleasant camaraderie and conversation, then I awoke.

In some ways the dream was disturbing, for my father has been gone many years now. And, it has been a decade since I retired from the bay, ill health and the depleted waters steering my course toward land.

I began putting the times of my life to paper about fifteen years ago, but found that after leaving the bay I could not write about it so soon. Reliving the times only in memories, the good as well as the bad, was too painful.

But I take the dream about visiting Dad on the bay for a good omen. It's time that the story of the bay is told, so that others can listen. I find myself seeing and hearing in my mind, my father, along with many others who played a role on the stage of my life. I hope to do them justice. I will tell my story as truly as I can so that my dreams may be good.

But more than that, it is my hope that the reader will become a friend and a lover of Barnegat Bay and her sister waters. The bay is neighbor to great numbers of people. I can't help but believe that if they got to know her, they would insist on a reversal of the environmental decline that has gone on for so many years.

I want the reader to see the bays and waters of our state with new eyes. I want them to see not just the day's weather reflected from the water's surface, but to catch a glimmer of its many different facets. Begin to see the bottom with its channels, the currents carrying many life forms. See the bay as a living organism, connected within itself, and to all of us. It is a part of our mother, the Earth, as we are.

We look in the mirror and see a single organism, but that is not so. Our bodies, like the bay, flow with many varieties of microscopic life. Some are so vital to our life functions that if they are destroyed, they must be replaced. It might be said that we are a small walking ecosystem composed of millions of life forms. The comparison between the bay and the human body does not end there. I have read that the salt content of our body is about the same as the salinity of the ocean at the time our ancestors emerged from the sea. Our blood is salty, like our tears.

When we look at the bay, just as when we look at ourselves, we should see complex systems that we are only beginning to understand. I am hopeful that the populace will come to see these waters as living entities whose complex biological mechanisms are failing because of human intervention. Hopefully the people will unite and make the necessary adjustments to correct what we are doing wrong.

To look at it another way, Barnegat Bay is like a great farm that some benefactor has left to the people around it to use for their own. Over the years the farm has developed problems. There are only a few baby cows this year. The rest of the herd is old. Most of the eggs of the ducks and chickens don't hatch. The apple trees in the orchard need tending, and the crop yield in general is bad. Because of this, the people who live around this great farm must import much of the food they eat.

In recent times the king, who lives far away, has appointed a committee of his ministers to manage the farm, with the result being years of decline. The people have not been allowed to vote or decide their own management. For the most part, the ministers have worn two faces — the one the public sees is a mask.

The people go to the farm to enjoy days in the fresh air, loving the sun and wind, and the pastures and woods. Life without it would be dull and drab. Only a few check the barnyards or crop lands and see what is going on. When they go to the ministers to complain, they are dismissed and sent home.

One man writes to the people — is it possible to awaken them?

Only time will tell, and so the story of the great farm awaits its next chapter, as must Barnegat Bay.

Perspectives

By the late 1950s, the environmental decline of Barnegat Bay was becoming dramatic, and easily recognized by seasoned baymen of the area.

When we start out to understand Barnegat Bay and her sisters, along with the inhabitants of the bay, we must bear in mind the word *perspectives*.

There are many perspectives from which to know Barnegat Bay. A philosopher would see the bay and her life differently than a scientist. A fisherman in a boat has a different perspective than a casual observer on land.

Let us look back from our time to the distant past. Thousands of years ago, when sea levels were different, tremendous wild storms struck the coastline of what is now New Jersey. They piled up sand and made huge dunes about a mile and a half offshore of the mainland.

Barnegat Bay was created.

The storms and tidal currents left a strip of water roughly a mile wide and approximately thirty miles long. The water, attempting to adjust its levels, created inlets, that were kept open by tidal flows. The inlets have a tendency to migrate southward. At times, nature closed them or opened them in her constant effort to adjust and improve on her work.

The flow of fresh water from mainland streams, along with the tidal flats (which over time became marshes) created an ideal habitat for many different kinds of birds, animals, fish and shellfish. It was a great natural hatchery, undisturbed by man until about ten to fifteen thousand years ago when the native Americans began to harvest and enjoy the waters and land that make up the ecosystems of Barnegat Bay.

The original people were good keepers. The early settlers found the bay to be bountiful. From the early 1900s, when coastal development really began, until modern times, there has been a great decline in the quality of life found in, on and around Barnegat Bay. By the late 1950s, the environmental decline of Barnegat Bay had become dramatic, and easily recognized by seasoned baymen of the area. If we were to use a graph, we would see a line that is fairly steady for thousands of years. In the last fifty to eighty years, it drops nearly off the chart. If it were the stock market, there would be a panic!

From this perspective it is easy to see that serious decline began around 1900. This trend intensified in the fifties and productivity of ecosystems in the nineties was at an all-time low. This is a red light flashing on the control panel.

The bay needs our help. At a music festival in the fall of 1995, I spoke to many folks, including well-respected baymen, who say conditions are worse than ever as far as stocks go. The waters themselves appear cleaner, which is a step in the right direction. However, it is only the beginning, for many environmentally harmful chemicals and other pollutants are being introduced into the bay from sources that we do not recognize.

I feel safe in saying that never before in the history of our bays has there been such an environmental disaster. This is one of many perspectives that I would like to show you of Barnegat Bay and sister waters.

Down 'Cross the Bays

I searched through my mind
on a cold winter's day
Looking for wisdom
The right words to say

But my words have no value
And little they're worth
To tell of these men
The salt of the earth

The west winds of winter
Blow down 'cross the bays
Drenching the workboats
In cold driving spray

But still there are smiles
And still there's good cheer
For it seems they grow stronger
This time of the year

You may see them in passing
all shrouded and grey
And ask why they're spending
Their lives in this way

It cannot be money
For look at their gear
Then watch as the sun sets
The answer is clear.

To some she's a lover
A mistress, a wife
To all she is home
And to all she is life.

A salute to the men of
The bays and the sea
Honest and strong men
Wherever they be

Now dusty old pathways
That lead down to the sea
On a cold winter's day
Are no place for me

But great is the value
And great is the worth
Of the men of the waters
The salt of the earth.

— Merce Ridgway, Jr.

A Young Boy of the Pines

To me, a boy of four years old who would one day become a bayman, the outdoors was a school that all native sons attended.

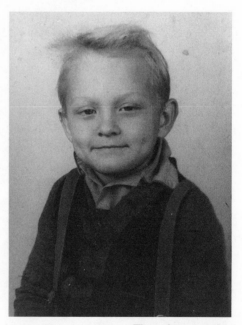

The author at age five.

The earliest memory I have is cloaked in a beautiful fall day. I have followed my father to a place in the woods where he is cutting pine. He kneels down on one knee, and looking me in the eye, says, "Stay within the sound of my axe, but not too close; wouldn't want a tree to fall on you."

These were thrilling words to me. It was the most gentle of tethers, leaving me free to wander through the pinelands of South Jersey and practice the new knowledge I was gaining of the land.

At first I watched from a safe distance the rhythmic and powerful swings as my father worked. With each blow of the axe, chips as long as my face flew high in the bright morning air. I watched and a certainty grew within that one day I would do the same.

Soon the lure of the woods beckoned, and I would wander off to practice the things my father was teaching me: to read the signs of life there, to forage for berries or look for lady's slippers to admire. The teaberry provided a snack and leaves to chew. A laurel cluster offered a place in the sun to dream. When I realized that the sound of the axe had stopped, I knew the direction to go, and headed back.

On the way out of the woods my father stopped for a few final lessons of the day. Kneeling down, he pointed.

"What made that?"

"A deer," I answered.

"Which way was he going?"

"That way." I could tell by the shape of the tracks.

"When?" my father asked.

I pointed to sand clinging to the pine needles in the deer's tracks. "Not long ago."

My father grinned and ruffled my hair and said, "You're doing great."

To me, a boy of four years old who would one day become a bayman, the outdoors was a school that all native sons attended. From these real teachings I would learn to draw sustenance from the land as well as from the bay.

▲ ▲ ▲

My memories of childhood from this point on seem to be a collage of unrelated events: clams that my father brought home lying in piles . . . the field spread with peat moss drying to be sold . . . big, mean snapping turtles in barrels being fattened for soup . . . tubs half full of fish that had to be cleaned . . . tubs of blueberries and an unbelievable contraption that actually sorted the berries, green from ripe . . . a garden full of things to eat, and my mother canning jar after jar, which we would open in the winter.

There was little sense of time in those years, only of seasons.

The chicks ordered from Sears and Roebuck would arrive even before spring had really begun, so they had to be reared under the brooder until they grew stronger. They provided a small income from eggs and a welcome addition to our diet. They also added to my education as I watched my father's constant battle with the varmints who wanted a poultry dinner themselves.

Spring brought a celebration of new growth to the earth. I knew it was spring when my parents set out to plow and plant a fairly large garden. This was another "native school" subject, adding seed to the ground and watching it multiply.

It seems to me that it was in the spring that my father went mossing. There was a lot of water in the swamps where he got the moss, so I couldn't go. But I could help spread the moss to dry in the sun when he came home. When Dad was ready to go, he put his moss drag and some other tools in the back of the truck. He came home with the truck loaded with wet moss. He did this several times and the half-acre field was full.

Dad built his own moss press. It was a device that used a big metal crank to squeeze the moss into bales. It had two doors about the size of a bale of hay. Out of pure deviltry, I locked my brother Dave in it one day. He was mad at me a long time for that.

Summer seemed to sneak up and one day all of a sudden, it was there. The summer showers would build up over the hot pinelands and come rumbling out over the bay, leaving rainbows and a young boy to wonder at where the storms had gone.

It was a time for catfishing at night from the dam at Bamber Lake with my dad and mom, time even for a dip now and then in the cedar water. It was a time for people to visit and admire each other's gardens; a time for me to chase fireflies, as the sweet sounds of music my people played filled the warm evening air.

The adults used to bring home the clams they had caught, and count and grade them in the shade, two clams in one hand, three in the other. With a rhythmic clack the clams dropped into the wire baskets.

Sometimes the people made little noises as they dropped them into the baskets. They would stop now and then and dump the basket of clams into a burlap bag. They called this counting. Made no sense to me, so I would wander off to dream of fall and rabbit dogs.

Fall came with a bang. The cleaning of guns was the first sign before that magic morning when father and uncles with their dogs would take to the woods and the sounds of barking and gunshot marked their trail.

Shots rang out more often at Grandpop June's, too. The young men and uncles Dick and Norman devoted hours to sighting and target practice. I didn't know it then, but in later years learned that the local boys referred to the place as Fort Sumter, because of the shooting that went on around there.

Amid all of that action, a young boy didn't want to be left out. I wanted to shoot, and I pestered my father. Dad cut off some shotgun shells, making them shorter and reducing the recoil, so I could shoot his double barrel Fox. I liked the .22 though, because it was easier to hold and easier on the ears.

Over at Grandpop June's one day I pestered the young men to shoot until they said, "Okay!" They loaded the .22 and I took aim. A small bird flew across in front of me. As I fired, it fell to the ground, dead.

"Did you see that? He shot that bird out of the air!" The young men stood there surprised.

"No," I said. "I couldn't have."

I hurt for the bird as I looked at the still form in the grass. It was an accident.

But the hunting season was about to begin. Soon the decoys were piled out. I loved the smell of paint as the men touched them up for another season.

Rabbits, quail, black ducks and mallards, brant, broadbill, butterball, merganser and geese all made the most wonderful trophy. All were to be examined and later eaten with gusto, for they were all very good to eat if you were a bayman's son.

Sometimes my father would load the garvey with his stool ducks and when the meadows were flooded during a receding storm, we would go up to Bullinger's Cove by Wrangle Point in Lanoka Harbor. When the stools were set out to his satisfaction, he would move the garvey a distance away so as not to alarm the ducks.

Then he would carry me on his shoulders across the flooded meadows to a duck blind he had built on a bit of high ground. Father and son spent some nice times together waiting for the ducks to fly in.

In the fall it was time to start cutting wood. Dad made good use of a circular cut-off saw and an old truck. One rear wheel of the truck was jacked up. We left the tire on and a large belt such as sawmills use ran on the tire. It had to have careful alignment with the pulley on the saw or it would run off. With this we turned logs into firewood for the cool fall and winter days.

Deadwood was a commodity free for the gathering by the pinelands native. Though there were those people who would cut or "outlaw" cedar, my father never cut a green tree. I knew at an early age that this was against the law.

I loved the sound of that old truck as it ran. The spinning saw blade slicing into the logs made a noise that could be heard for a long distance, ear splitting, but exciting. I have never gotten over the nostalgia that old trucks and saws evoke in me, perhaps I never will.

Fall was the time for cranberries brought home by the hunters, and frost-ripened persimmons, sweet and juicy. Fall was also bittersweet, for the cold winds spoke of winter to come and frost chilled the ears and nose.

Winter settled in like a cold blanket. Snow covered the ground and the piles of firewood, but inside, rabbit stew simmered on the stove. I liked this season least, for outdoor activity was too often canceled. I was too small to be out much. Only vague images of snow and cold survived the childhood winter years, along with traps and muskrats and boards for skinning and stretching. My father's trap lines provided extra income in the winter, not to mention that pot-roasted muskrat was a gourmet meal to the native. Muskrat is dark meat, sweet tasting and tender.

▲ ▲ ▲

Life, it appeared, held many wonderful activities that a person might take part in when he grew up. If there was one thing I most wanted, it was to have a boat to go out on the water. I don't know why, I just wanted to.

By the edge of the field between our house and Grandpop June's there was an old boat. It was a pretty large sneakbox, it seemed to me, and remembering it now, it must have been eighteen feet long. Even though she was old, she was all clean inside because she'd never had a motor in her. Evidently they had sailed it at one time.

I loved to crawl inside that boat and inhale the fragrance of old cedar. That smell was better than anything I could think of. There is something special about an old boat that has been out in the bay in the salt water when she sets upon the land. Funny thing about that particular scent those old cedar boats have.

I was five in 1946 in my earliest memory of Barnegat Bay. My father had an ancient sea skiff. Chugging sedately out Forked River creek was a dreamlike experience, which turned into a sort of nightmare as my father opened up the motor to full throttle on reaching the bay. The roar of the engine, the flying spray, the vibration all conspired together to scare the wits out of me.

Seeing that I was upset, he slowed the boat down. I quickly recovered to enjoy the gleaming expanse of bright blue water and sparkling sunshine.

There were no houses in sight and the dunes at Island Beach seemed to beckon with a golden glow. I was fascinated not only by the water but by what must lie beneath the water. I thought perhaps sunken pirate ships and golden treasures might lie there. I was overcome by a passion to know and explore the vast body of water, but this would come later.

▲ ▲ ▲

My father played the guitar and sang, and I knew that he went away to play on the radio station. In the late afternoon there was a train that passed through a field across from Taylor Lane, the road in Forked River that we lived on. It was a steam engine, towing passenger cars down to Barnegat. When that train came by, I knew it marked the time for me to go in the house and listen to my father.

We had a radio that operated off a car battery. I remember peering through the holes in the radio at the glowing tubes inside. It seemed to me that if I looked hard enough, I certainly ought to be able to see him.

It took some time for me to realize that he wasn't actually inside the radio. I was always sad when the program ended and he was no longer with us. I loved the music and felt strongly that I wanted to play also.

Another great thrill as a child was to ride in Uncle Roe Taylor's horse and wagon — the wheels crunching on the road, the clomp, clomp of the horses' hooves, the creak of the harness, the musty smell of the horse — the magic of it all! Maybe when I grew up I would get one.

▲ ▲ ▲

Toward the beginning of one bright fall, a new word entered my vocabulary — "school." When I asked them to explain this word to me, what school was, they said it was a place where I would learn the things that I needed to know about life.

Well, I was already learning the things I was interested in and didn't want to go anyplace with a name like school. They told me I had to, regardless if I wanted to or not.

I decided that I would resist, and climbed up a big old tree in the back yard, determined to stay there until it was too late to go to school. As time passed I began to realize that this form of resistance had some inherent problems. First, I began to get bored. Even worse, I got hungry. So, at last, defeated by myself, I climbed down out of the tree and began to think about other ways that I might avoid this outcome.

As that fateful day approached when I would be taken to this place called school, I still had not come up with any method that held any hope. That sunny day when they had me all shined up to go, I locked my arms around an appropriate tree in the front yard and hung on for dear life.

At first I thought I might win. My mom and Aunt Eldora talked calmly to me and told me it was no use, to come along peacefully. This only encouraged me, for I thought them perhaps too weak to pull me away from the tree, and so they must be trying to trick me into letting go.

This stage didn't last very long. I thought I was pretty strong, but I was no match for a pair of determined ladies and soon found myself deposited in the back seat of the car.

We soon arrived at the little two-room schoolhouse in Forked River. They marched me into a room that was half-full of crying children about my size. This was not a good place to be.

Things went uphill from that point on. School did hold a few small miracles. Lo and behold, the lights in the ceiling came on when the teacher pushed the switch. No one I knew had electricity. And there was running water that came out of faucets without a hand pump, a commode that flushed — mysteries indeed!

We got along without the modern amenities. When I was born, my parents lived in Bamber, a long way from the paved surface of Route 9. Taylor Lane in Forked River, where we moved closer to town, was more or less a gravel road. When it rained there were huge mud puddles to pass through. Even on Route 9, the traffic was light, more like a country road. The woods in back extended all the way to the bay. Across the highway you could walk ten miles to Bamber and not find a house or cross a hard top road.

The house we lived in was a wedding gift to my mom from her mom, Pheniah (They called her Nina). She had inherited it from Uncle Bird Taylor. In later years Mom and Dad sold the Taylor Lane property to buy land and build a house in Lanoka Harbor. If another Depression came, there would be public transportation and they would be able to get to the doctor's or to the boat.

A new stage in the future bayman's life would begin. Lanoka was to be the place where I would grow to young adulthood and at eighteen, from where I would go off to see the world. Many happy times were had with brother Dave and sisters Judy, Elaine, Kathy, Muriel and Faith.

Dad cleared the land by hand, and family members, including Grandpop June, pitched in to build a frame house. The well was driven by hand and soon we had water. Over time Dad hooked into the electric which ran by on the highway.

Electric lights in the house for the first time! Water, pumped and heated! Radios you plug in! How rich it seemed. But it really marked the end of a simpler era.

At right, fourteen-year-old Merce with his first hunting license. Below, Merce and Streak in an old rowboat on the meadows.

24

Bayman Beginnings

The bay gave to those people who worked there good times and bad times — to quote one of my father's songs, "A lot of making do with what you had times."

As a small boy, I would go out on the bay with my father as he worked tonging clams. I'd spend the day fishing from the cabin top, climbing down to grab any broken clams to use as bait for my hook.

I mostly caught little black sea bass (not to be confused with tautog) and, at certain times, silver fish we called spots or grunts for the grunting sound they made when they were hooked on the line. Some days I caught as many as a half-bushel. We cleaned them and put them in the freezer for the winter.

We carried on board tarred lines with wire leaders and red and white feathers for catching bluefish. The tar prevented the lines from rotting, and the feathers worked fine as rigs. That's all it took; you could catch all you wanted in those days.

On the way home, I would steer from the stern and work the trolling rigs as Dad counted and graded the day's catch, which he washed and dumped into brown burlap bags for the dealer.

I was always sorry to wind in the lines when Dad was finished. Washing down the boat meant the day on the bay was over.

At the dock we would unload the day's catch into his truck to be sold, and then it was home for chores and food. By then, like most small boys, I was ready to eat.

I never dreamed the time would come when the sea bass and grunts, tarred lines and red and white feathers would be a thing of the past, preserved only in the minds of the natives.

Sometimes we would go over to the sedge for soft crabs. We would take inner tubes, place a bushel basket inside the hole and wade the shallows. The water was crystal clear with no grass. We could plainly see the crabs scurry out when we poked the crab net into clumps of lettuce, which is a type of seaweed they would hide in.

Care had to be taken with soft crabs. If placed in the same basket with the hard crabs and shedders, they would be eaten before we got them to the dock. They also had to be removed from the water and wrapped in damp lettuce or they would become "paperbacks" and continue to harden.

The hard crabs were boiled and eaten within a day or two. The shedders we kept in wooden bait cars at the dock, checking them every day to see if they shed. Then they made a delicious sandwich. The ones we didn't eat were used as bait for weakfishing in the evening.

There were big fish roaming the bay in those days. One night, fishing from our sixteen-foot garvey in the bay off Forked River, a large fish — I often wondered if it was a shark — thunked the hull hard enough to knock me off the deck backwards into the boat. Dad had been sitting on an overturned bushel basket. Now it was splintered and he was on the floor, too. He thought that whatever it was smelled the shedders in the bait car. We never knew for sure. It ended our fishing for that night.

▲ ▲ ▲

The biggest problem, as time went by, was that I became physically ill with pain in my joints and my back. A couple trips to the hospital in Red Bank couldn't seem to find the problem. The adults began to credit my discomfort to my strong resistance to being incarcerated in school.

By the time I was seven, my worsening condition brought a diagnosis of rheumatic fever, which for me turned out to be two worse words than school. At the age of seven, I had to go to bed, there to remain, they told me, until my body temperature returned to normal.

No activity whatsoever that involved body use was permitted. If I cheated when no one else was looking, the fever would be higher in the evening and my mom could always tell.

So, the only recourse was reading. My aunt Viola and my uncle Augie brought me boxes of books from their attic. I read constantly.

One beautiful book as I remember was entitled Charles Darwin's *Evolution of Species*. It was large and had many black and white prints and illustrations. I read it many times as I lay there and marveled over the ideas that this man was unfolding in front of me.

This ended one day when I told my father about these ideas. I little expected the consternation that this book would create where I lived. My people were Christian God-fearing folk and felt the ideas projected by Darwin were contrary to their religious doctrine.

To my dismay, and to Charles Darwin's had he been there, the book was to contribute to the household heat as it joined the rest of the kindling in the stove.

But, I still had plenty of other books to read and eventually the day came, about a year later when I was eight, that they declared my body temperature had stabilized at normal. They said I could now begin to sit in a chair and walk very slowly for short distances. I began to pass the time now by playing an old ukulele, sawing on my Grandpop's fiddle and sometimes playing Dad's guitar, or attempting to.

During this time period they told me that I had a heart murmur and might never be able to work normally.

I had learned through some of my reading that the heart is a muscle and that muscles can be strengthened, so I began to plan for my recovery. I followed instructions to the "T" until I was about nine. Then I began casting about for some ways to go to work and earn my own money. My parents resisted the idea. I told them that I would sooner be dead than be helpless for the rest of my life.

I told them if they would let me, I would grow stronger. I talked a local farmer, Harry Gray, into giving me a job hoeing corn for ten cents a row. My dad and Harry talked about it and it was agreed that I could do this as long as I would stop working when I began to feel tired.

So, for the first summer I would hoe nine or ten rows of corn until I began to feel fatigued. It was a rewarding and helpful exercise.

Although I loved the farm, the tractors and the trucks, the growing things, and Harry and his wife Hazel were so good to me in those years, I wanted to be on the water.

The summer I was ten I told my parents that I wanted to go to work with Dad on the bay and catch clams. Because I had responded so well to the first year of work, Dad gave me an old pair of tongs and put me in the boat.

The first day, sitting off of Wrangle Point, which is just by Stout's Creek in Lanoka Harbor, he told me the rules were the same. I could work, but only for short periods of time to begin with. I caught a hundred clams that day. At a penny apiece, I made a dollar, which was equal to hoeing ten rows of Harry Gray's corn. Each time I brought the tongs up, I fully expected to find, along with a clam, some of that pirates' treasure that I dreamed about.

That summer he continued to take me with him and I caught as many as 300 clams a day. I was earning two and three dollars a day. I never seemed to tire of it, and grew stronger.

By the time I was fifteen or sixteen I could catch between 1,200 and 1,500 clams a day. A grown man would average 1,700 to 2,000 per day.

At this age I began to go on the bay in the colder months of the year. The first of November was the opening of scallop season. For us it was a small family business. Dad and I would leave the docks early in the morning and be in by ten or eleven with thirty or forty bushels of scallops.

After lunch my mom, dad, brother and sisters and I would start shucking in a small shucking house Dad had built in the back yard, where we would work until nine or ten at night. The hours were long, but we didn't complain. Even my smaller siblings would lend a hand in the final cleaning of the white scallop muscles. Many times we wouldn't get them all shucked. Mom would shuck the next morning sometimes as many as fifteen bushels, as I remember.

They would be finished when we would show up with another thirty or forty bushels that afternoon. This would go on at least through November and December.

If there were crabs, Dad might continue on the water for a while in the bitter cold months of the year.

I'll never forget those early days on the water with the ice forming on the fronts of our rain gear, and us out there pulling our crab dredges on Barnegat Bay.

▲ ▲ ▲

The brant came down the bay in those days in huge flocks. They would land in the gunners' decoys or fly past. If the gunners knocked down one or two birds, brant would fly around and still try to land again. Sometimes the circle was completed, then broken, three or four times. We had little law enforcement in those days and they shot them by the gunnysack full.

Up until I was about ten years old, the bay would yield her fishes to me, while I innocently watched my father work.

Like the blind man who felt the elephant's side and said it's like a wall, I only saw a part of the picture. The rest developed before my eyes as I grew to begin making my own living.

At around seventeen, I learned that there were other aspects that had not been so obvious to a young boy, but would affect my perspectives for the rest of my life as a bayman. The most prominent of these aspects was state management, which at that time might more accurately have been called state mismanagement. To the casual observer, it was not obvious. To an intimate of Barnegat Bay it could be considered a sort of a rape.

When school was out in the summer of my thirteenth year, Dad told me we would be going down the bay, as the clams around Forked River were disappearing. Neither he nor I suspected that the planes, which flew out of Forked River spraying DDT, were the cause. I remember him pointing to the iridescent colors in the oily slick from their spray and remarking on their beauty.

He took me with him when he moved the boat, and we stopped at Van's, a seafood retailer on the Manahawkin causeway. We worked there, north of the Manahawkin Bay Bridge, into July or August. The clams from there turned green inside and could not be sold. "We have to go further south," Dad said. Cedar Run was the next stop.

It took me several years to realize that according to the map makers we had left Barnegat Bay. It seemed such a continuous strip of water in my mind, and I felt it was all part of one great bay.

I will never forget that summer out on Cedar Run flats. I found many of my relatives working there: my Grandpop June, my uncles, Fred, Walt, Dick, Norman, Tommy and Herschel; my grandmother, Nina; and my aunts Eldora and Dot.

They were all tonging clams.

Although I should have known, I didn't realize that some of the women in the family would be out there working. Giving fair credit to them, they sometimes caught as many as or more than the men did.

Grandpop June had a long, low garvey. It was narrow, with a wood stove in the cabin. It wasn't uncommon at lunchtime, particularly on cooler days, to see the smoke come puffing out of the chimney.

And so all together like one big family, we had all left Barnegat Bay to work on the Cedar Run flats. I had to agree that it was a far better place to be working, for now I could catch 600 or 700 a day, and there were many small seed clams that we threw back.

We kept a crab net on the boat to harvest some of the constant procession of crabs that swam by, big hard crabs and doublers (hard crabs carrying either shedders or soft crabs).

My father had a clam lot off Forked River and he began dumping the seed clams on his lot in hopes that in the fall or the following spring, they would be large enough to sell.

He built a small clam stand in front of our house on the highway. It attracted a good business. Those that were not sold after an appropriate time were also thrown on the lot to be reharvested in the winter months. We kept a small garvey in Forked River for the purpose of going out on these lots to dump and to retrieve the clams that he had placed there.

I will never forget the look on his face, when on one of these retrieving expeditions he was unable to locate the clams that should have been there. Even more strongly I remember the feelings I had watching my father and one of his lot mates as they took their guns at night to wait for the outlaw who was stealing from them.

Those days were lean and hard for the baymen. I knew that we depended on those reserves that were so diligently placed there. As I lay awake at night, part of me wanted them to shoot the thief, and a part of me was apprehensive that my father might be shot in turn.

They never caught him. A part of me was sorry. A part of me was glad. I would become sour on the state's leasing system and the lax marine enforcement that wasn't there to help us when we needed it.

Each passing year was to give me a better understanding of Barnegat Bay. I began to know her in her many moods.

I saw her when she was calm and lovely. I saw her stir in agitation when the northeast wind blew with a fury and hurricanes came up the coast. The tides would come up, flooding over the meadows and over the access roads, causing the baymen to tenderly care for their boats and be in fear of losing them. I saw her withdraw when the winds blew out of the west and the ice froze to the decks.

I learned where the scallops lay in the fall of the year, and in deep waters where the crabs bedded down for the winter. The oysters grew on the northern end of Barnegat Bay, toward Good Luck Point. The bay gave to those people who worked there good times and bad times — to quote one of my father's songs, "A lot of making do with what you had times."

▲ ▲ ▲

The year I was seventeen, oysters became plentiful in the upper bay toward Toms River. I pleaded with my folks to let me quit school. I brought home my textbook, showed them that they were teaching me Darwin's Theory of Evolution. Thanks to Charles Darwin, I escaped from the school system to go oystering.

My father didn't exactly encourage it, though. He told me he felt the bay was failing; it was no longer a place for a young man to plan on spending his life. My parents wanted me to get an education that would lead to a normal job and well-paid happiness.

But I had defined my own goals and I knew what I wanted to do. I wanted to work on the bay and be a successful musician. My father had tossed aside a career in music to retreat into the bay and woods. I cherished music and would not throw it aside. Meanwhile I was walking the woods for miles, looking for the perfect place to buy to build my house for the woman I would love someday.

As far as the bay failing, I thought it was doing better; the oysters were coming back.

Oystering was a new and exciting experience, although somewhat marred by bad politics and other problems I will elaborate on further in this writing.

It was at this point in my life when I told my father I wanted my own boat. I was earning good money. I wanted to be independent. Dad said that until I was twenty-one I would stay home, work out of his boat and that I had no choice because that was the law.

He had the right to make that decision, but I told him I thought it was unfair. Sadly disappointed, I began looking for a means of escape.

Some bright-eyed young girl in a local ice cream parlor said, "Why don't you join the Marines?"

I hadn't even considered such a thing. All through school they said that my heart murmur persisted, and so I had not been allowed to take part in sports.

I was determined that I had nothing to lose and just maybe I might be able to sneak in.

On December 29, 1959, at eighteen years old, I went to see the recruiter in Atlantic City. He gave me some tests and told me that I had missed only two or three questions; when would I like to leave for Parris Island?

I was thrilled. I told him, "As soon as possible."

He said he would pick me up for physicals and more tests on December 31st. If I passed, I could leave that night.

Nine o'clock on December 31st found me in his car and I saw Philadelphia for the first time. That evening, New Year's Eve, they put me on a train and I was on my way.

It was a classic case of jumping out of the frying pan into the fire. I rode the train south that night with thoughts of new futures and new woodlands and wetlands to experience.

They had given me a temporary M.O.S. (occupation) in artillery communications. I was still fascinated by electricity and radios.

I saw the Marine Corps as an organization full of strong and fearless men that I would emulate.

There was a big party on the train that night, for it was New Year's Eve. I was somewhat startled as bottles of alcoholic beverages appeared all along the train. Everyone except me began drinking. At first I was amazed and then it began to amuse me, for the people around me became ridiculously silly. A blonde woman about thirty-five started kissing all us young boys bound for Parris Island.

As it grew closer to twelve o'clock, they became more and more ridiculous and inebriated. Round about me, my fellow future Marines joined in the festivities. One or two got dead drunk immediately. Some of those young fellows were experienced drinkers even at the tender age of eighteen. They held on longer. Round about midnight, everybody on the train jumped up and started hollering, "Happy New Year!" and kissing and hugging.

I fled the cars on the train where these functions were taking place and made my way to the sleeping area. I lay there with dreams of the new woodlands that I would see and soon fell asleep.

Awareness came with a harsh voice grating in my ears, "Alright, Marine, fall out!"

It was the drill instructor. He was a big burly guy. He looked a little like Yul Brynner, from what I could see sticking out of his Sergeant Preston hat. His voice sounded like he had a pair of pliers for vocal chords. He had the same look on his face that Harry Gray's bull had when he got mad.

Needless to say, the discipline of home life was mild compared to Parris Island.

The Marines in those days rebuilt you physically and mentally. It taught me many of the same things that my parents had, in regard to honesty, honor, duty and country.

Four years later, the Marines sent me home with a lot more confidence. I got out in a cold, snowy winter. I was doing masonry work for a bachelor's wages. I needed to get my head straightened out — it takes awhile to adjust. I felt I would do better money-wise on the bay. Last, but not least, I cared not to work in town or on the land.

The water calls, a siren song.

chapter three

The Boat

*I didn't know it then but I was about
to embark on journeys powered by a lot
of different motors. Some I would love,
some I would hate, and even the good
ones wear out.*

I was just starting out, and I had to have a boat. The six-teen-foot garvey that Dad built lay down at the township docks, along with a couple other boats the locals had stored there.

She hadn't been used in a while, so I had some work in front of me. My wife Arlene (joy of my heart), whom I had recently married, came to help.

Together we caulked, nailed, puttied and painted until the boat was ready.

I bought a used outboard motor, got together a basic kit — tongs, anchors, and the rest. Now I was ready to run the boat to Cedar Run where I would tie up.

The trip down was pleasant. The boat was dry; the motor was iffy. I didn't know it then, but I was about to embark on journeys powered by a lot of different motors. Some I would love, some I would hate, and even the good ones wear out.

An old motor is better than no motor, and so it is with this account of my life, for telling it is proving no easy thing to do.

▲ ▲ ▲

I knew when I went to work out of the sixteen-foot garvey that it would never do for the winter. I started thinking about building a boat of my own.

When I went off to the Marines, $100 would build a cheap boat; $200 or $300 would put you into a good boat. By 1964 the lumber for the sides alone added up to $200 or $300. The motor, hardware and fittings would cost hundreds of dollars more.

I figured that if Sam Hunt in Waretown could build one in a week, I should be able to build one in a month. This was a month I really did not have, as I had a wife and family and needed to produce.

So I started looking for a boat to buy. The average vessel on the market was about a thousand dollars. I went up and down the shore, looking. Most of the boats I found weren't what I wanted.

At the Cedar Creek Marina, I found a boat that came within inches of the plans I had drawn up of the boat I wanted to build.

The garvey was called the *Fin, Fur and Feather* and had been the main boat for the gunning club of the same name. She was 25 feet 9 inches long, with about 8 foot 9 inches of beam. The boat had a V bottom and a tunnel; it would operate in about twelve inches of water. She had a Chrysler Crown engine that looked as if it had been cared for.

The boat had been out of the water for some years and needed lots of work, but the price was right — $250.

The garvey was a duck hunter's dream and a bayman's nightmare. The main cabin covered almost half of the boat, with a windshield and an overhanging roof that extended back another six feet. The boat was set up so that it could only be operated from controls that were installed on the cabin wall.

Inside the cabin were bunks, head, table, stove and other gear that the duck hunters had used to make themselves at home. I had grown up on the bay, and I had no doubt that such things had no place on a workboat.

I went to work and stripped the boat. I took the monster cabin off and everything that went with it — the windshield and the overhanging roof. The mechanical steering was far too stiff to ever steer from the stern. That went, too. A fellow came along and asked what I was going to do with it. "Take it," I said. "I have no use for it."

He thanked me, and over the years he gave me many hundreds of feet of surplus rope, from the company that he worked for.

Once I had the boat down to a bare hull, it was time to start the motor. To my surprise, it started right up and sounded fine. It had no water in the block, so I shut it down until the boat was in the water.

I caulked for about a week, and painted the boat on the outside. The next step was to run water in the boat and start the swelling process. It had been a dry summer and the boat had not been in the water in some years. It had a lot of leaks, but the marina owner said not to worry, we could hang the boat in the slings of the travel lift until she swelled up and could float on her own.

By now we were well into October, and scallop season was close. We hung the boat in the slings in the water, and it took three days till she would float overnight without sinking. It took about two weeks till she stopped leaking altogether. When I started the motor with water in the block to cool it, I found trouble. The motor missed badly, and a teardown revealed a cracked block. Bob Laureigh, who was the mechanic for the marina, had a bare block. He worked with me all night to get the parts from my motor on the other block. I put the motor back in the boat, and started down the bay the next day.

I used the boat for about three years, and it was clear that she suffered from the curse of all old garveys, her nails were rusting out. A galvanized nail has a lifetime of about eighteen years, and the boat was about twenty-one years old.

When they get like that, they tend to leak as long as you are using them. When the boat sits, it tightens up. The flexing of the hull causes it to start leaking each time you go out on the bay.

As soon as I was able, I pulled the boat out of the water and turned it over.

I stripped the hull down to bare wood and covered it with $^3/_8$ inch plywood. I used gallons of Weldwood glue under the plywood and one ring nail per square inch to fasten the plywood to the hull. I then covered the plywood with about thirty gallons of fiberglass resin and three layers of medium-duty fiberglass cloth. Our son Tom was a great help and Arlene also pitched in. It was a big job and I still remember and appreciate their help.

I now had a strong, leak-proof boat. A little at a time I added new decks, ceiling (as the baymen call the floor), and a pilothouse, which went in the center of the boat.

I had many different motors in my search for the best, but small block Chevys and the 318 Chrysler gave me the most dependable service.

It cost a lot of work and a good deal of money but I had a boat that I could count on. I could break ice a foot thick and go out when the wind blew. Best of all, I could go long distances in a short time.

The boat would carry all that I would catch over the rest of my career as a bayman. It would bring me home when other people would not think of going.

I would spend many wonderful days on the bay in her, and I still take her out in my dreams.

Baymen I Have Known

They were the men who played a major role in shaping my ideals of what a bayman should be.

Sam Hunt building a boat in 1979.

The bay provided most of a bayman's income in my younger years. What didn't come from the bay usually came from the garden or the woods.

Nowadays this version of a bayman can rarely be found along the Jersey Shore. A new version of a bayman has taken its place. I should say

39

bayperson, for women go forth on the water also.

In truth, anyone who begins to love and appreciate and understand the bay begins to be a bayman. It is only a matter of degree from amateur to professional.

I came to know a great many baymen over the years who made strong impressions on me. A few of them made an impact on my life. They were the men who played a major role in shaping my ideals of what a bayman should be.

▲ ▲ ▲

Thomas Taylor, Jr.

June, as he was known locally, was my maternal grandfather. He is credited for making the first clam tongs with metal teeth. Wooden teeth were used preceding this and were not as durable.

He sailed for oysters in his youth and took part in most of the occupations that a typical bayman would during his lifetime. He told me that during these early years the oystermen depended on getting their drinking water from the mouth of the Forked River. This is a clear example of how much the environment has changed over the years.

He was also a musician, playing the fiddle, spoons and the mandolin. His brother, Dewey, told me that he played a tune on the fiddle the first time he ever picked one up. He was best known for playing the mandolin, however.

▲ ▲ ▲

Merce Ridgway, Sr.

Dad was born in Barnegat, but his father, Joel Haywood Ridgway, Jr., moved the family to Bamber during the Depression. His father found work in the peach orchards that were being planted there. He also worked as a guide during the hunting season.

One morning my father was watching some members of a party prepare for a hunt. One hunter was having trouble getting his gun open; it was supposed to be empty. The gun fired, hitting my father in the leg at close range. Dad was about four or five years old at the time. He was about fifteen before the wound healed. I never heard him complain, though he walked with a limp from that time on.

The beach was only fifteen miles away, but it was a big fishing and shellfishing adventure for Dad as a youngster. He would often talk about the big weakfish, ten or twelve pounds. Frost fishing was another story — in the fall when the west wind blows and the temperature is low, the whiting come up in the surf. The surf will throw them up onto the beach. They're chilled by the air and have trouble getting back in the water. They called that frost fishing.

Dad learned to play the guitar, and performed with Bill and Walt Britton. They called themselves the Pinehawkers. They enjoyed moderate success playing on early radio and television shows, at the National Folk Festival, and other locations.

Although the Pinehawkers stopped playing out, my father went on playing and writing music. In 1990 Marimac Recordings of Little Ferry, New Jersey, produced a tape of his songs.

He settled on the bay early on as his primary occupation, although he worked as a machinist during the war and as a carpenter for the WPA (Works Progress Administration, a program instituted by President Franklin Delano Roosevelt). During off-seasons on the bay, Dad mostly worked at traditional occupations such as mossing, woodcutting, trapping, and building his own boats. He approached the outdoor work as if it were a regular job, consistently working regular hours as much as possible.

My father was religious and honest. I never saw alcohol in the house, and although he gave up smoking when I was quite young, he had a heart attack and stroke at fifty-three while out working on the bay. The doctors gave him six months to live. He lived another eleven years, thanks to the good care my mother gave him. Those years were probably his best years for writing and playing music.

Dad said one time, "When the wind blows at night, I wake up and hear it. I start to worry about my boat, and then I realize I don't have one." I was never sure if he was glad or sorry for that.

▲ ▲ ▲

Roger Wilbert

Roge, as he was called, was one in my grandfather June's peer group from the Forked River area. He worked on the bay till advanced old age.

I stopped to talk to him one day off the south point of Forked River, and he began to tell me about the Barnegat Bay of his youth. "The bay was full of things to catch," he said. "There were no clams where we are, all oysters, all the way up the bay. This is nothing. They killed the bay, the oysters, clams and the fish."

He then proceeded to describe how bad politics from the past had allowed Barnegat Bay to be raped, as he called it. Then he repeated the story of how it all happened. It was a story I had heard many times before from other sources and which I will tell you before this writing is done.

He was a burly, outspoken man, an honest straight shooter who feared no one. I truly loved to visit him out on the bay.

▲ ▲ ▲

Edgar Barkalow

Edgar was a big fellow with a genial way about him that made you like him right off. He and Dad were friends and often worked out of the same docks together.

He built a fish and clam stand and sold from there for a while. Like my Mom and Dad, who also had a roadside stand, he found dealing with the public not to his liking, as it was a sometime thing.

Edgar was a hard-working, all-around bayman. During his life he railed against politics of the bay, but he was always ready to laugh at a good joke.

I saw him off Wrangle Point shortly before he passed on. "I'm glad that I'm not a young man with a family," he said during the conversation, "the bay is getting so poor."

Not quite sixty-five, he was gone a few days later. He never saw the Social Security he was waiting for.

▲ ▲ ▲

Bernie Penn

Another big, strong man, and very vocal, he was not afraid to speak his mind and tended to let you know what he was thinking. Bernie was a hard worker and one of the few baymen to catch grass shrimp, which he sold to party boats. Like his brother, Frank, he worked the bay for whatever was in season.

He was also, as near as I can determine, the only authentic bayman to serve on the Shellfish Council which governed baymen's activities.

A friend of my father's, and a distant relative of mine through my maternal grandmother, Pheniah Penn Taylor, I remember him as a rough, but good-hearted man.

He had a pacemaker implanted and worked the bay for a while afterward, eventually to fall to a heart attack.

▲   ▲   ▲

Ern Penn

It was said that in his youth Ern was an excellent bayman, but being a bachelor and not needing the money, he was content to catch eels and soft crabs in the Forked River.

When I would meet him, he would give me a look and say, "You know how to get 'em, don't you, boy?" I knew to answer back, "corn," for it was a standing joke.

He could skin an eel faster than anyone I have ever seen. Often we would meet at the top of the tide as we went along Forked River Creek, catching soft crabs. We always talked and went on our way with friendly feelings.

▲   ▲   ▲

Sam Hunt

Sam Hunt is undoubtedly one of our most famous baymen.

He enjoyed freedom early in life. At eleven years of age, he was running his own boat out the inlet to fish. He holds the all-time speed record for building a twenty-six-foot inboard garvey. He got the lumber on Monday and went clamming out of it on Saturday.

It would require a large book to tell all about Sam. He is a musician and builds banjos, tables, chairs, sneakboxes, and other things out of wood. His craftsmanship has been recognized by the Smithsonian Institution. Sam's knowledge of the bay and the woods as they were in the early half of the century is extensive.

One of the musicians from my father's generation, I spent many happy hours playing music with him. I looked forward to meeting Sam at festivals and such.

Russell Horner, Sr. at work on the bay.   *Joe Reid in his workshop in Waretown.*

▲ ▲ ▲

Russell Horner, Sr.

When Russ talked to you, he exuded a personal force that you could almost feel. Russ was articulate and a writer also, penning a column for *The Beacon* called "The Old Timer."

I recall one cold morning, we were sitting in the truck watching the ice on the bay. "There were two houses in the area that is Forked River Beach," he said. "We lived in one during the Depression. In the fall, we would walk down by the bayshore and the scallops would be piled up in windrows on the shore, by winds and tides. We would carry home all we could to eat. No place to sell them in the Depression, and you can only eat just so many scallops." This is an invaluable picture of how productive Barnegat Bay was at one time.

▲ ▲ ▲

Joe Reid

Joe was a well-known maker of clam tongs, a bayman and a builder of boats. He served as the mayor of Waretown for many years, and introduced me to *Robert's Rules of Order*, a book that was to be very important to me in years to come. A founding member of The Baymen's Association for Environmental Protection, he was an excellent source of counsel to me in that endeavor.

He was a wise and considerate man and is greatly missed by us all.

▲ ▲ ▲

Hurley Conklin

Hurley was a genial, easygoing man. We tied our boats next to each other at the Cedar Run docks for a year or so.

He told me once that he had never worked for anyone, spending his life working the bay and carving decoys.

One day at the docks, he said how amazed he was at the decoy trade. "Why, I guess I could have been a millionaire if I wanted to."

As proof of his excellence, both as a man and a carver, awards are given in his name at the decoy show each year in Tuckerton.

▲ ▲ ▲

Paul Lafferty

Paul was like Hurley, in the sense that he knew how to take a fishing pole and go fishing when it was time. He told me once that if I wanted to last, take some time off and go fishing once in a while.

Paul worked the bays up and down our coast and was a well-liked and experienced bayman. When I knew him, he had a V-bottomed garvey that would run through the ice without completely breaking it, leaving a narrow strip where the shaft and rudder cut.

He was a guide in his youth and well spoken of by all who knew him.

▲ ▲ ▲

Herlan Cornelius

Herlan, or Blue, as he is called, is one of the best baymen around. He is a hard and consistent worker, well-respected and well-liked by all who have known him. Like most of the baymen I am writing about, he has worked the bays as the seasons dictated. The first light of day found him on his way out the creek, a late start being almost a lost day.

Also an avid gunner, he guided parties for ducks and is an excellent carver of decoys.

▲ ▲ ▲

Dolph Hall

Early on, I moved my boat to Burton's in West Creek for a time, and there I met Dolph. He used a shinnecock (sometimes called bullrake or big rake) with the old wooden handle. He was the first raker that I had met who could catch clams really well. He encouraged me to use a shinnecock, and I did acquire one and use it as time went by.

▲ ▲ ▲

Norman Dupont

Norman is an excellent all-around bayman. He has a good eye for shape and form and builds a beautiful boat.

As a fellow musician — he plays the fiddle — I used to enjoy talking about music structure and philosophy with him out on the bay.

He told me once that he worked algebra problems in his head to pass the time as he worked out on the bay.

▲ ▲ ▲

George Camburn

Winnie, about my age, was another man known as an excellent all-around bayman, like his father before him. We spent many years working the same areas and shared many a laugh out on the bay.

A hard worker, he went down to the Carolinas for a while, though I heard later that he was working in Jersey again, doing well, I hope.

▲ ▲ ▲

Rocky Wycoff

Rocky was a sharp, interesting man. He was known far and wide for his ability to project his voice. Baymen need strong voices to talk to other workmates over the distances involved on the water, especially when the wind comes up. He had the strongest voice of anyone I ever knew.

He kept a neat, fast boat and was well liked. Catching me barefoot in the boat one day, he told me, "Always wear something on your feet." I laughed, for in thirty-nine years I had never hurt my feet in the boat. That night at the docks, I sliced my toe on the scratch rake. He taught me to protect my feet.

▲　▲　▲

Art and Jack McNemer

Otter, as Art was called, raised a big family, mostly off of bay work. As I recall, his children were all girls, and, like my girls, they went on the bay with him and could all run and operate the boat.

His brother Jack, like Art, was good-humored. They would do whatever they could to help anyone out. The last word I got, they had moved to Carolina and were still working on the water.

▲　▲　▲

A few more family members worked the bay. My brother Dave, my uncles, Fred, Dick, Norman and Tom were all fine baymen, along with our son, Tom, who grew up on the water.

Many of the buyers of shellfish worked the bay also. They included the Ahearn and Cottrell families in Waretown, and the Larsen, Cranmer, and Conklin families in Cedar Run. There were others, but I dealt mostly with these people over the years. They were all good people and worked hard. They fit my first description of a bayman and were part of what is now a vanished lifestyle.

Above, a picnic on the bay beach during the sixties. Left, Tom Gille at age 14. Below, Arlene Ridgway with her banjo.

chapter five

Family Ties and Times

*Those were the good old days and I
knew it, even back then.*

When I married Arlene, I gained an instant family —
she was a widow with four children. I was in love with Arlene, and her
children were the nicest I had ever met in my life. And, if you love children and treat them nice, they tend to love you back.

Tom (Robert T. Gille, Jr.) was the oldest, then Cathy, Virginia and
Wendy. They are descended from the Gray and Gille families of Forked
River and Waretown. Their birth father, Robert T. Gille, owned a sea
skiff and fished commercially offshore.

Their grandfather, Leopold Gille, Jr. (The senior Leopold had a party
boat out of Forked River Yacht Basin), was a pioneer in regularly fishing
the Gulf Stream about seventy-five miles off the Jersey coast. He sailed
from Barnegat City and counted Babe Ruth among his patrons. As my
son Tom remembers, "My grandfather took the Babe out fishing for
giant tuna every year. The funny thing was that my grandmother's nickname was Babe, and that was the name of Leopold's boat, the *Babe II.*
My grandmother told me that Babe Ruth was a very nice guy. They always had a good time with him when they went fishing, and when he

would come to dinner at the house."

So, with that heritage, Tom was a natural on a boat. We decided when he was eleven that we would buy him a rowboat. When we got it home to Laurel Lake in Barnegat Pines, we tied it up to the bulkhead. The boat had come with no oars, but we'd have to take care of that later.

The next morning I left for work. I stopped in at Ted French's bait shop for something I needed. The phone rang. It seemed that Tom had found something to paddle with, and took off for his first cruise.

Arlene was frantic. "He'll go over the dam!"

"No way," I assured her. They sold oars there. I would get some and come to the rescue.

Tom's cousin, Eddie Wilbert, was working there at Ted's. He'd heard the conversation and was laughing. He handed me a pair of oars and said with a big grin, "These are for Tom."

Tom and the boat were soon home safe and sound, with Tom a little wiser to the wind of the lake. It turned out that he had drifted nowhere near the dam, but straight across to the other shore.

From the beginning, Tom helped with boat maintenance and dug right in whenever there was painting, scraping or motor work to be done. He started early on to go with me on the bay and worked hard at learning to catch clams and scallops.

In the summers when he was around age thirteen he started mating for his uncle Tom Gray, a well-known striped bass specialist who sailed out of Forked River.

When duck season came in, Tom and a couple of his friends wanted to hunt. Tom got a small duck boat, which we loaded up with decoys.

We would tow this rig to a point in or near my work area. Once there, I would help them build a blind and set out the decoys. The blind we made out of whatever we could find on the bayfront — old boards and reeds, seaweed and marsh grasses.

This done, I would go to work out on the bay and watch them as they hunted. I remember one morning down by Long Point, when the birds flew so good that they had their limits before I ever reached my work area. I just made a circle and helped them pick up. Those were the good old days and I knew it, even back then.

One night after dinner Arlene said to me, "Cathy has something to ask you."

"Sure, what is it?" I replied.

"Can I go out on the bay with you?" she asked, with a hopeful look about the eyes.

I was startled! None of my sisters had ever wanted to go to work with Dad. I tried to explain this, to no avail. This was the liberated sixties; girls could go to work any darn place they wanted to, including the bay!

"How about your aunts and grandmother?" Arlene asked. "They go out on the bay; aren't they girls, too?"

I was won over by their logic, and we really did want them to be strong and capable women, prepared for life as fully as possible.

As we had with Tom, we approached it as if it were a real job, so they would get 10 percent of whatever I made that day.

I came to appreciate their help. They would throw shells and vegetation overboard for me as I worked. They fished and read, and we talked a lot and had fun. They ran the boat as I counted off my clams on the way home.

Each girl handled the boat differently. Cathy would steer straight and true for home.

"I enjoyed the freedom I felt running the boat across open water," Cathy now recalls, "and the smell of the bay and just being completely surrounded and embraced by nature."

As Ginny steered home, I would hear the motor song change as she pushed the throttle ahead - just a little, soon a little more, and then we'd be planing.

I would turn around and yell, "Slow the boat down!"

With a redheaded grin from the pilothouse, she would slow us back down.

"Dad knows what my favorite thing about the bay was. Driving the boat, and going fast!" laughed Ginny. "I would help, and steer out of the crick (where you had to go slow because of the other boats), and when we got out to the bay, I don't know if he actually let me, but then I'd get to go fast, until he would give a look, and slow down I did."

Wendy was next, and by the time she was six or seven, could steer a straight course home. She used to take bags of pencils, pens and other art supplies with her; they had lots of spare time, and she loved to draw and write.

Wendy remembered, "I loved to go out on the bay with Dad. He would teach me about the clouds, the wind, the water, the birds and the sea life, and all the things that I loved. His skin was always so brown, his hair bleached by the sun, and he'd play his guitar for me out there on the water. What more could you want."

In 1966 we added another daughter, Amber, to our family. She went out with me from about age five. She'd get bored running a straight course and tended to wander off to explore things, zigzagging our way home.

"Slowly, we'd chug along the creek," Amber remembers. "My excitement grew as we got closer to the bay. Out of the mouth of the creek we'd go and into the expansive bay. The speed would pick up. Dad's eyes were intently on the horizon, his ears tuned to the engine's music, listening for any discordant sound. When all was well with his observations, he'd point to some far-off distant landmark on the other shore. It may be a hill taller than others, a buoy so far out it looked like a pin on the horizon, and he's say, 'Go towards that'."

In 1968 came another daughter, Jennifer. She went out with me from the time she was around five or six years old, and tended to lock onto the course home.

"I loved it. It was a chance to earn money and get a tan at the same time," Jennifer told her mother. "It was fun being with Dad, and I had fun learning about all the little creatures that came up in the rake."

Our children started going out on the bay — family boat rides and picnics — when they were infants in bassinets. I took them out to experience a ride on water, but only on beautiful weather days.

From the time they were toddlers, they loved to turn the steering wheel, regardless if the boat was tied up at the dock or on the bay, anchored. The boat whistle was a particular attraction to all five girls. Amber loved to sit on the bow deck and play that whistle for hours. Boat whistles have three notes, which never resolve themselves! (Those dissonant three-note whistles were intended as a signaling device, not as a musical instrument.)

Jennifer was born during a violent east windstorm clocked at eighty-seven miles per hour. The wind took the top off the marina building on Oyster Creek and carried it about 200 feet to land on a bunch of expensive boats. The tide was over the meadows. My boat would have sunk — I spent the night in Lakewood Hospital waiting for our daughter to arrive — had it not been for fellow baymen Art and Jack McNemer and the other good men down at South Harbor in Waretown. They pumped and kept my boat floating until I got there in the morning. I was home late and woke up about daylight, and heard the wind howling a gale outside, but no rain. I thought it had shifted off and I thought the wind was from the west. When my phone rang, I found out it was blowing due east and my boat was in danger of sinking from the spray that the wind was blowing in from the bay.

"I have that old boat in my backyard," Tom said recently. "One day I plan to rebuild it, because it was the finest garvey on the bay. It could hold a big load, plane out easily; it drifts properly and was comfortable to work out of. And, by the way, Merce was the best clammer I ever saw. He would always beat me, and most everyone else, too. He could smell the clams. He could find good spots and always figure out how to catch them, and catch them he did!"

▲   ▲   ▲

The bay was a big help with our diet. We ate often from the bay — shellfish, ducks, crabs and fish. My wire basket usually had something in it at night, if only a small fish for the cat, which learned quickly to look there for her treat. The cat didn't trust crabs, however, and her antics would make us all laugh as she tried to get her fish out of the basket with a couple cranky crabs guarding it.

We had a salt water fish tank which we stocked from the bay. One mid-sized crab lived for some time. Now and then it would escape and walk around the house, mostly at night, a fact which most of the girls

(Arlene squawked the loudest) did not appreciate. Most often it seemed he would guard the refrigerator and the entrance to the bathroom door. There were night lights in those areas, and I think he went for the light. As I remember, Tom did most of the maintenance and work involved with this project.

As the youngsters grew, I was rewarded as one after the other, they started to play musical instruments. I remember at one point we only had one guitar to share between us. The guitar sang constantly. It had no name; we bought it for nine dollars. One of the children, I don't remember which, put a Chiquita banana sticker on it, and from there on it became the Chiquita. As more instruments came, Chiquita made the rounds in the family; she traveled a bit, she did.

As time went by, we acquired other traditional instruments - the mandolin, fiddle and banjo. Everyone played them all to some degree.

The family grew through the music. Jon Foreman lived down the street in Sands Point. He became Tom's good friend and married our daughter Cathy. He played the guitar at a young age and was at our house a lot — his home away from home. We all had many a grand old time with music. We cooperated as a family, and there was love and respect.

I am happy to report that there still is. When we see one another, there is good food, good conversation and good music.

chapter six

The Dark Side

My father used to say, "It seems like, if anything is going to happen, it happens when the wind blows."

Under the summer's hot sun, the bay is peaceful. A few fishermen are drifting the channel looking for fluke. Seven or eight sailboats are moving slowly along in the light east wind. Off to the west, over the mainland, float a few mushroom-like clouds. They are low on the horizon, and to the untrained eye they don't look the least bit threatening.

One o'clock is early, but the baymen are already starting to count and grade their catch. Now and then they cast a wary eye toward the west as they work.

By 1:30 the clouds have grown to black thunderheads and the first rumbles of thunder announce themselves. By 1:40 most of the baymen are headed for home, some of their boats showing surprising speed. The wind has died out completely and the towering thunderheads now cover the sun. The sailboats that were ghosting along are now starting their auxiliary motors and furling their sails. One or two are running up storm sails. The fishermen along the channel have disappeared in a howl of outboard motors. I am working on upper Barnegat Bay and cutting it to the edge, as they say: it is now about 1:45.

I know my garvey will run about thirty-five miles an hour and I have a good pilothouse to take refuge in, so I am not overly worried. From where I am in the middle of the bay, I need only minutes to reach the lee shore, off the south point of Cedar Creek. I am about 200 yards offshore when the wind hits like a wall.

The boat shudders and heels; I heave to. The howling wind and water have reduced visibility to zero. The land has disappeared in the howling storm. There is nothing to do but watch the compass and hold on slow ahead.

I can't believe my eyes. A child in a canoe has appeared out of the storm.

The boy is hanging on to the gunnels with both hands.

I am his only chance, and it is an amazing twist of fate that I am there. My mind races to beat the storm's thoughtless attempts to sweep the boy in its clutches. There can be no mistakes. I must reach him on the first try.

I steer the boat so the canoe, which is broadside to the waves, passes close enough to grab. The wind is driving the rain and spray sideways at fifty or sixty miles an hour and the waves are three feet high. Why the canoe has not capsized I do not know.

As the canoe comes by in a series of lurching tosses, I throw my garvey out of gear, go out the pilothouse door and lean far out to grab the canoe's bow.

Got it! It takes only seconds to get a rope on the canoe, and then I can feel the boy's arms around me as I bring him aboard.

It's into the warm pilothouse with the boy and me; by now we are both soaking wet. The storm is still raging, but for us both, the worst is over, even though we've been blown farther from home and the boat is plunging and leaping into the five-foot seas.

"How are you doing?" I ask the boy.

"Okay," he says, still shaking.

His eyes are as big as saucers. I pour some coffee from my Thermos and fish some cookies out of my lunch pail.

"Want a cookie?"

"Sure," the boy says with a grin.

"Didn't you see the storm coming?" I question.

"Yes, but I didn't know it would get like this," he replies.

I tell him, "Get off the water when you see a storm coming."

"From now on I will."

By the time we are inside the lagoon at Laurel Harbor, the sun is out and two anxious and relieved parents are waiting for their boy and his canoe. I head on home with a sense of purpose about life.

Only a summer squall, but a very real look at the dark side of Barnegat Bay.

Intense squalls come with the territory along the Jersey Shore. They should be watched for and avoided if at all possible — it's much too late in the middle of one to find out it's bigger than your boat.

The squalls seem to occur most often around the change of the tide. The reason for this is unclear. Another feature of those storms is that they always move into the wind. Rising columns of air pull more strength into the storm as it approaches. When the storm hits, the wind comes from the opposite direction, sometimes with great force.

I was caught off Cedar Creek one day in a storm whose winds were clocked at eighty-seven miles per hour. It blew boats off their cradles at the marina. I thought I might perish that day. That much wind feels like a giant hand pushing your boat down into the water. All you can do is hold your boat slow ahead into the seas and pray your bilge pump or something else doesn't fail.

Another peculiar thing about these storms is that just before they hit, the clams always seemed to be up. That would tempt us to work until the last possible minute before running for the lee shore. Under the shore's protection I could run home with relative ease.

▲ ▲ ▲

One day the sky was black and angry, and I was speeding home under the banks by the game farm beach. I was watching a sailboat as she made her way from the bay into the mouth of the Forked River.

The wind struck with violence as the storm moved out over the bay. The sailboat — she was twenty-six or twenty-eight feet — heeled over on her side as the top of her mast disintegrated. From my position I could see someone fall into the water. A life cushion was thrown, but the wind carried it 100 yards past the overboard man.

The gulf between him and the safety cushion widened and the sailboat could not maneuver in that wind to pick him up.

Once again, it became my turn to see what I could do. No other thought ever crossed my mind. The problem was much the same as with the boy in the canoe. Whatever was done had to be done right the first time.

The two or three hundred yards separating us were now a solid sheet of wind-driven rain and spray. Under these conditions, an object the size of a man's head was nearly impossible to see.

Once I got closer and spotted him, there were other considerations, not the least of which was to bring the boat alongside the overboard man without running him over or hitting him with the propeller. As I circled around for the maneuver, I hung a rope sling from my stern for him to grab.

It worked perfectly. As soon as I saw him grab the rope, I threw the motor out of gear and was out of the pilothouse and back to the stern. Once he had his foot in the sling, I was able to hoist him aboard.

I looked around for the flotation device. It was long gone.

We made our way back to the sailboat, which had its motor running. The man's mates were hard at work on the wrecked gear. I transferred him to the sailboat and went on my way.

Needless tragedy nearly occurred twice because a few simple rules were broken. The man was not wearing a life preserver. The boy was wearing a waist belt-type flotation device.

Wear your life vest, particularly if a storm is coming. Seek shelter, a lee shore will do — remember the old adage, any port in a time of storm. New Jersey's coastal waters comprise a wonderful natural treasure. But on the water, as in so many other cases, we need to follow the rules and treat the water with respect.

One early fall day I had worked down by Beach Haven, and was on my way up the bay to Cedar Run. The wind was about twenty-five miles per hour, blowing up a storm from the south. As I came off the flats by the north point of Shelter Island, I could see some wreckage out by the main channel. It seemed kind of strange, so I went to take a look.

I could see something sticking out of the water. It looked like a fair-sized pole. Floating nearby was a pile of sticks.

My boat was rigged so I could steer standing outside the pilothouse. The door was also hinged, so that if I stood behind it my body was protected from the weather.

Between bursts of spray I had a clear view of what was ahead. That thing sticking out of the water made no sense at all. The dark mass nearby was starting to look like the wreckage of a boat, with no signs of life. Had it been floating free I would have turned and gone home; I was not interested in salvage. The fact that a stake anchored it interested me. I had never seen anything like it. As I drew closer, I could see that it was a boat.

I was about 200 yards away when I detected movement. The man I saw first, the woman second. They were clinging to a wrecked catamaran. About four feet of the mast was sticking up out of the bay. The rest of the boat was anchored by the stays, which were still attached to the mast, which somehow had been driven into the bottom of the bay.

The first priority was to get those people out of the water. The waves were three feet high and the wind was still picking up. I brought my boat around and made fast to a downwind corner of the wrecked cat. I hung a rope sling from the stern cleat, and the man, being a gentleman, began to assist me in getting his wife aboard.

All this was taking place as the two boats banged and crashed and we bobbed up and down with the waves. Blasts of cold salt spray, driven by the wind, broke on us every few seconds. I was warm and dry, however, almost waterproof with my foul weather gear on.

In spite of our best efforts, we couldn't get his wife in the boat. This was no time to be gallant. Let's try it with the husband in the boat. He was in still in good shape and had no trouble hoisting himself up. When she got her foot in the rope sling, we both pulled, and finally she was in the boat.

"Thank you, Great Spirit," I said to myself.

I got them into the pilothouse, telling them, "I'm warm and dry, you get the same way."

I got on back to the stern and let the rope out about ten feet, so the boats weren't beating on each other. I can't stand that.

I stood in the stern for awhile, and looked at the wreck that I was fastened to. What really fascinated me was the mast, which was driven into the bottom of the bay and was holding the whole mess in place.

After a decent interval, I returned to the pilothouse and opened the door. "How did you do that?" I asked.

"Pitch-poled," the man replied. (It seemed to me that was when a sailboat turned completely over.)

"I thought that could only happen in deep water," I said.

"Not so, that's why the mast is driven into the bottom," he answered.

They seemed in good shape and were most appreciative of my services. They asked if I might tow their boat in. I kind of liked that idea, for I was interested in how hard that mast was driven into the bottom.

I made sure that we were fastened well, started the motor and put the boat into gear. Nothing happened, it took considerable power before the stays broke and the wreckage came free.

We idled over to Long Beach and had a pleasant chat en route. Turned out he had built the boat himself, and if I caught his wallet in my rake he would be very happy. I said I would return the next day and try to pull the mast out of the bottom. I towed them to Beach Haven and went home.

I did return the next day and put a rope on the mast. It broke off about two feet under the water, leaving me with about six feet of mast. Since I had only a part of the mast and no wallet I never called the couple back.

The use of high visibility flotation devices would have made them easier to spot in the water. The area where they were wrecked could not be seen from the main island because of intervening Shelter Island. They were out of sight and there were no other boats in the area.

I liked to work in the wind, for the energy it gave me to pull my rake through the bottom. As a consequence, I was on the water when few others would be, and that's when things happen. These waters are very rough when the wind blows up or down the bay. Boats that have dirty or waterlogged fuel tanks, loose wires and/or faulty mechanical gear tend to break down.

My father used to say, "It seems like, if anything is going to happen, it happens when the wind blows."

▲ ▲ ▲

The largest class of rescues in which I rendered assistance was that involving mechanical breakdowns. A great many breakdowns were off Cedar Creek in Barnegat, but most of them were off Wrangle Point.

I would see a boat come along, plunging and leaping into the seas, and the forward motion would cease abruptly. As the breakdown occurred, the operator would climb out on the bow deck and throw the anchor overboard, and nothing would happen. The boat would continue on its way, the wind and waves driving it toward the banks or bulkheads.

Not only are they broken down, but also they have a second problem. They can't control the boat or stop it. The boat may be worth thousands of dollars, but their only insurance against this situation is a twenty-nine-dollar anchor better suited for a rowboat.

In the days I was on the bay it was a legal requirement that all boaters render assistance when another was in distress. That meant I must pick up my gear, clear the decks (didn't want to lose my catch overboard) and disassemble my rake. Then I would run to the broken-down boat and get a line to them, before they were in a position where I could not maneuver.

At times when I could not get to them because of shoal water or other reasons, I would anchor bow to the seas and float a line in to them, using a couple of life vests or a five-gallon can. Once I had a line on the grounded boat, the tricky part began.

The bow anchor line would be taken in until it was judged about to pull free of the bottom. At this point, I would return to the pilothouse and put the running motor into gear. Just enough power would be applied to break the anchor free, and I would begin to pull the troubled boat. The weight of the chain on the anchor would keep it from hitting the propeller, as long as we went slow. Once we cleared the hazardous area, I could stop and bring the anchor aboard the boat.

None of the boats I pulled off the meadows and such would have been there if they had the right anchors to fit them. If you can anchor your boat with authority, that is, with little or no problem, any time, anywhere under any conditions, you have the right anchor for your boat. If it is big enough, a second anchor of the same size, rigged and ready to go, would be the minimum anchoring requirement for any boat.

I was working in the cove north of Stout's Creek one day when a young man in an old beat-up garvey came along. He said a friend of mine had sent him to me, saying that I would help him out. This friend turned out to be a man I had heard of, but never met, and I was wary. The bay was failing but the boy was making the step into manhood. I told him he was somebody's boy, so I would help him out.

It was not too long before I saw something. The boy was wearing laced-up hunting type boots. I told him to leave them home. "They are too hard to get off and might drown you if you fall overboard."

I told him to get a pair of rubber boots two or three sizes too big. Rubber boots that fit tightly seal to your feet when they fill with water, and are very difficult to remove. Rubber boots that are too large let water and air pass around the foot and the boot can be removed much easier.

The time passed and a few years went by. That young boy grew strong and muscular, a fine young man. He sold his garvey and bought a skiff, a net boat to work the ocean in.

One northeast day in Barnegat Inlet, he capsized. It was so fast and unexpected that his shoulder was dislocated as he was holding the steering wheel. Yet, he and a friend who had gone with him managed to swim out of the pilothouse and from under the overturned boat.

He told me about the accident and said, "Had it not been for those loose boots, I would have drowned. I got my boots off fairly easy, but my buddy nearly drowned getting his laced boots off and he did not have a dislocated shoulder."

Sometimes it is the little things that count. Listen to your subconscious mind. It is better to err on the safe side.

Swede Lovgren told me something years ago that stuck with me. Swede was coming in Barnegat Inlet one day and he found himself in a position where his boat, a clam dragger, was sinking. "I didn't know what to do," he said. "So I just started throwing things overboard. Pretty soon, the right thing to do came to me and I saved my boat."

"Merce," he said, "if your boat is sinking and you don't know what to do, do something, even the wrong thing, and the right thing to do will come to you."

Something tells me this is a good time to end this chapter on the dark side. If this information helps someone some day, I will be well rewarded. There will be more of the dark side as we go along; you will know it when you see it.

Above, seed clams. Right, a day's catch in the clam rail of a garvey. Opposite page, a shinnecock rake.

chapter seven

The Hard Clam

*When I got my dollar bill that night
I realized that I did get a treasure from
the bottom, clams.*

The common hard clam, also known as a bivalve or sometimes quahog, is known to the scientific community as *Mercenaria
mercenaria*. The Ridgway line comes from ancient Mercia in England,
and my common name is Merce, as was my father's.

I have read that the hard clam is millions of years old and has pretty much stayed unchanged over time. I found clams that had petrified on Parris Island in South Carolina. The island had been backfilled and the dredge spoils contained many clams that had turned to rock. I knew it took a long time for that to happen. Most were broken up, but a few were in such good condition that they could almost be mistaken for live clams.

Clams live roughly forty-five years. The areas where they are found are regulated by the salinity of the water. The lower the salt content, the less chance of finding clams.

In the spring, when the water reaches a certain temperature, hard clams begin their spawning activities. If successful fertilization occurs, the larvae rise to the surface and are moved about by wind and tides for two weeks. At this point they drop to the bottom and attach themselves to grains of sand, shells or other debris.

I learned in high school that the hard clam has a *pseudopod,* or false foot (we called it the tongue), which it uses to move up and down in the bottom. This observation, an accepted fact among the baymen, was not embraced by the scientists who studied the bay during my time. They thought that clams just sit there like rocks in the mud. Clams are also credited with lateral movement, which I also feel is a fact.

Clams are filter feeders — they siphon in the water that contains their food and filter out what they eat. Mostly they like to eat decaying vegetation that is generated on the marshlands and carried out on the bay by the tidal action.

The clam has sustained generations of my family and others. I was about ten years old and had talked my father into taking me tonging with him one fine fall day. It was to be my first attempt to use tongs. I was recovering well from my bout with rheumatic fever and I was very excited to be going to work on the bay.

My father had an old worn-out pair of tongs that he had cut off. This, along with some planing of the wood handles, made a pair of shorter, very light tongs that a boy could use.

We worked off Wrangle Point that day, and the 100 clams I caught that day were worth one penny each, so I made one dollar — not much by today's standards, but a lot in 1950. It was the start of what would be my primary occupation for many years to come.

That spring some bottom came soft and I started tonging off Barnegat with my dad. I worked on Saturdays and days off from school from that point on. I loved going out on the bay, and always thought I would find a treasure in the waters.

One day the men were standing around the docks talking, and I was hanging out with my ears open, as small boys do. One fella was leaning on the hood of his old car.

"Did you hear about so-and-so?" he asked. "He caught a gold brick tonging, over to such-and-such a place."

I was about five years old at the time, and I fell into a dream. Gold from pirate ships . . . I would find it one day, I felt sure.

And so, each time I felt the teeth of the clam tongs hit something in the hard bottom, I thought it might be that gold bar!

When I got my dollar bill that night I realized that I did get a treasure from the bottom, clams.

The hard clam was king when I was a boy. Once only a lowly resident of the bay, cast there by the connoisseur taste of the oyster-eater, the hard clam was assuming new importance to the bayman. The oysters and soft clams of my grandfather's time were gone. Oysters did experience some recovery in the late 1950s, but the hard clam was truly king.

Around 1959, an article appeared in a national wildlife magazine that would turn out to preview the clam's rise to prominence. It told about the brant, a small subspecies of the Canada goose, which winters only along the Jersey, Delaware and Maryland shore and a section of the California coast. The number of brant was down, so the biologists were planting grass, which they had brought from California waters to try and supplement the diet of the brant.

They planted this grass on the flats over by Sedge Island, which is where our present day grass problem started. I refer to it as a problem, because the grass didn't stay there.

But the grass helped the hard clam to become king — it began to grow at the rate of about a mile a year. As it sent its roots into the bottom, it softened the soil of the bay and collected silt.

Many things happened. Most notably for the shellfisherman, the hard sand bottoms of many flats became soft and silty.

Now the older populations of clams could be felt by stepping on them, and treaders began to have a field day. The tongers didn't like it much — the grass got in the way of the tongs and made for a dirty boat.

The younger sets of clams seemed to like the edges of the previous year's growth of grass and set there with great success. As time went by and the grass took over, we could see that clams did not set well in spots where the grass was well-established.

Fortunately, the hard clam is a very tough animal. He lives and prospers over a wide range of conditions. I have found him in nearly forty feet of water at the bottom of deep channels. He lives up in the meadows in small creeks. The loss of the flats as habitat, as the grass spread, did not affect the clam as much as it did other resources because of the clam's ability to tolerate a wide range of conditions.

▲　▲　▲

There are a few basic ways to catch a clam.

Start with treading. To be a treader you need at least one good foot to feel the clams with. I know of two men who regained the use of a paralyzed leg and credited treading clams as the therapy that worked.

You need something to put your clams in. We used an old inner tube, which we had placed a bushel basket in. Some treaders use clam cars, which are small boats or rafts designed to carry more clams.

You need to protect your feet as the bottom is full of hazards — conch shells, rusty cans — who knows what you are apt to run into out there. Most treaders used to make their own boots out of inner tubes or canvas.

Once you have your boots and your basket with its floating inner tube, you can proceed to the area you wish to clam in. Hopefully, you have checked your maps and license, are in shallow water, and in an area that the Marine Police approve of.

Go overboard gently (remember the conch shells). Feel with your feet; if you're lucky you might feel a small lump in the bottom sand. Digging with your toe, roll a clam out, which you can reach down and pick up to throw into the basket.

Progressing from this simplified method, the art becomes more and more complex.

I recall tonging in the lee of an island south of Ship Bottom on a cold and windy winter's day. Over on the beach, a treader had parked his car and put his wetsuit and other gear on. I watched him wade into the water, towing his inner tube and clam basket. He reached the channel and started to swim. I was having a hard time keeping warm with my insulated gear on and this man was swimming around in the water! He swam across the channel and worked until the tide started to rise, at which point he swam home. He had perfected his gear and his physical condition to the point that he was able to do such a thing.

▲ ▲ ▲

The scratch rake was a common tool on the bay before the grass on the bottom made it almost useless, constantly plugging up the tines. In my early days, the flats were clear and scratch raking was in vogue.

At sunrise in the summer, we would already be on the bay. By ten in the morning, it was getting hot.

The gnats and flies would get bad if the wind did not blow at least a small breeze.

It had to get real hot to get my dad in the water. When it reached a certain point, he would sit down on the rail, swat at the bugs with his hat and drink water. We always carried a gallon jug of well water from home. Sometimes the jug of water would lie up under the bow deck for a while before we needed it. When we got it out, the iron and sediment would have settled to the bottom. It would be cool from the night before, and the sweetest water in the world on a hot summer's day.

At this point, I would lay it on about the cool water of the bay. I wanted overboard in the worst way, and Dad knew it. "Okay," he would say with a grin, "I guess it's time to get your basket and tube, and throw your scratch rake in the water."

We would tie a short line on the basket and flip the clams out of the rake and into the basket as we worked. As soon as the wind came up a little, we were back in the boat. The tongs are a much faster way of collecting clams.

Tonging was the method preferred by most baymen in my youth. The tongs were made up of three important parts: the handles, or stales, as they were called around Tuckerton; the pin, which was the fulcrum point (the support for a lever); and the heads, the part of the tongs which actually contact the bottom and catch the clams.

The handles were made of pine for many years, until mahogany became easy to get at local lumberyards.

We made all our own handles. Dad would start by selecting a board that fit his idea of what was needed. He would select the board for strength, weight, type of grain, and of course, the length. All this was to construct as light and strong and responsive a handle as possible.

If you tonged much out on the bay, you would soon have a favorite set of tongs. One day they would break and you knew it was time to make some handles. You always broke one of the two handles; the other, being somewhat stronger, survived. Now you had a pattern to use for your new stales. It was marked out, a little full to allow for wear, on the board that we had selected and roughly sawed out. We then hand-planed and shaped the wood until it was the proper size. It was critical that the area of wood to be in contact with the hands be well-sanded and clear of any plane ridges. Even well-calloused hands will blister and become quite sore from rough handles.

If we had remembered that our tongs have a left and a right handle, we could clamp them together and install the pin and plates. A general formula for pin height was about two inches for every foot of handle you were making. This varied somewhat from bayman to bayman. I have seen tongs where the pin had been moved several times as the owner tried to find the optimum position for his pin.

The brass plates were inset after the pinhole was drilled, and copper rivets were used to hold them in place. The pin in this case, a brass bolt with two washers and a nut, was installed. We tightened the nut to about where we wanted it, and cut it about $1/8$ inch long. The bolt was peened (bent or rounded over), much like a big rivet to keep the nut from working loose. The heads were adjusted so they closed properly, and were bolted on. If we had done our job well, we were ready to go to work.

When you first went to work tonging for clams you would become sore. All those muscles that you used working and lifting those tongs hurt. This would last about two weeks and then you would start to break in. Your hands got hard and your blisters healed. You started to feel strong and looked forward to the next day. It was an ordeal that must be repeated each time you went back to tonging after a change in occupation.

▲ ▲ ▲

Using the shinnecock is another method of catching clams. I have seen a drawing of men raking clams in Princes Bay off Staten Island in 1869. It is an old method of clamming that was much improved in the last thirty years. The handle went from wood to metal, and the rake evolved into a highly efficient catching machine with refinements such as adjustable sleds to control working depth of the teeth, and weights to increase rake speed through the bottom.

Different sized rakes are used according to the type of bottom worked, and the preference of the men working the bottom. I used rakes having from sixteen to forty-two teeth over the years; twenty-two teeth seemed to be a good all-around size, however.

The assembly of a modern big rake is a complex activity. The water depth and tidal flow regulate handle length, while bottom conditions dictate how the rake is used and set up.

There are a few other ways that clams can be caught, such as gathering cut-outs (clams that are exposed by the ice and tides along channels and such). They are the exception rather than the rule, and we will deal with some of them as we go along. Of course, illegal methods such as pole dredging did exist. Never having done that, although I've seen it done, I will not describe it. I can say that people who engaged in that type of thing were not well liked by the baymen in general.

▲ ▲ ▲

The clam is a survivor, but he can only take so much.

If you let him get so cold that he has ice inside, he will most likely live when you thaw him out. Sometimes we thawed clams that were frozen and found they were still alive. These were clams that had been in our home freezer for some time. I used to like to put some clams in the refrigerator early in January. I would lay them on their side, so they would retain their body fluids, and they would live for about six weeks, more or less, depending on their condition and holding temperature.

The clam does not like heat. He will expire before your eyes on a hot day if left in the sun. Until you can refrigerate him, keep him cool, in the shade, and wet if possible.

All baymen carried a wire basket to wash the clams in. After the clams were sorted and counted, they were washed one last time in the waters of the bay. The bayman would lower the basket of clams over the side of his boat, and shake and roll the basket of clams in the water until they were clean.

Now and then we might run into a dealer who wanted a special sorting of the clams. Most of the time, we graded the clams into three sizes: 'necks, cherries and regulars. Small clams under one-and-one-half inches in size, called peanuts, were thrown back into the bay, as they were illegal to keep.

I have read that man is the worst predator the clam has ever encountered in its millions of years of living in the bay. The clam is eaten by conchs and starfish, attacked by drills, and subjected to the fury of storms and tides. But man is the supreme predator, because his pollution often kills what he does not catch.

M. mercenaria still survives. Long live the king.

chapter eight

The Crab

Crabs can communicate. It was well known among the baymen that if you went to work too early on the crabs, they would get up and walk away.

The crab is nobody's friend, but somebody is always looking for him — many people like to catch and eat him.

The crab is well named, for to call his disposition crabby is a bit of an understatement. In the summer he will bite you faster than you ever thought anything could move. A big old blue claw in the prime of his life can be a real test of one's ability. Until he is in the pot, he will do his level best to get you.

The first experience with crabs that I can remember was many years ago on Barnegat Bay. I think I was about five or six, and my father had towed a rowboat along to the place where he was working. When we got there, he put me and my lunch, along with some crabbing gear, into the rowboat. He anchored the rowboat and moved his big garvey a short way off, where he anchored it up also.

He wasn't far away and I had a life vest on. If I fell in, he could fish me out.

I loved being there. My crabbing gear consisted of some string, some cracked clams and a small crab net. The net portion was made of wire; it is much easier to get a crab out than the cotton or nylon nets that tangle in their claws.

I tied the string onto the shell of a big chowder clam that I had broken. The remaining shell acted like a sinker and carried the clam to the bottom as I let my line out. The crab will eat everything he can find that is composed of animal protein. We used about whatever was handy, which most often was clams. The crab loves mossbunker, an oily fish, and many people use chicken backs.

I sat there in the rowboat, holding the line and lifting it gently now and then. Soon the tug on the line was stronger. I began to pull the string in very slowly. If it is pulled too fast, the crab will drop off. As it neared the surface, the white glow of the clamshell soon showed, along with the white of the attached blue claw.

Soon he was at the top of the water. The crab was so engaged in eating the clam that he did not seem to notice that he was about to be captured. Holding the line in one hand and the net in the other, I scooped him up and dumped him in the boat.

He was furious and big. His two giant claws waved in the air as he headed in my direction. The rowboat was small and I didn't have anything to catch him with but the net, which would not fit under the seats because of the wire basket. Dad offered to come over to catch him, but I turned him down. I was going to let no crab take over my boat. I hopped from seat to seat as the crab stalked back and forth. I cornered him in the bow with a stick. The crab bit the stick with its enormous claws and hung on. Then it was easy to lift him and shake him into the bushel basket.

I was only a small boy, and small boys need a challenge to overcome now and then. I really could not see what my father found so funny about the whole deal!

Later on, he showed me how to step gently on the crab from behind with the toe of my foot and immobilize him. Once I had done that, I could reach down and pick the crab up by the rear flipper. The crab is not double-jointed and cannot reach either back flipper. You may safely pick up a crab by grasping the back flipper where it joins the body at the back of the shell.

I learned in school that the crab has an exoskeleton. In other words, his bones are on the outside. Nature really did two jobs with the crab's shell. It serves as a skeleton and as a defense, as its many sharp points appear intimidating.

The crab is much like a person with arthritis who cannot raise his arms higher than his head. In order to get his claws up, he must raise his body up on his legs and tilt it back. This works out well, as it gives the crab a very threatening posture.

▲ ▲ ▲

The male blue claw is easy to spot by the bright blue colors he sports on his claws, legs and flippers. If you turn him over, you will see a T-shaped strap or pouch on the bottom of him.

The lady crabs are easy to spot, too. They wear red fingernail polish on the tips of their legs and flippers, with more red polish on their claws. If you turn a female over, you will see a larger, darker and more rounded pouch when compared to the male crab's pouch. This is where she carries her eggs.

Crabs do not grow as you or I do, a little at a time. They shed their shells when it is time to grow. During the time when they are preparing to shed, they are known as "shedders." They are somewhat more difficult to pick out, but with practice it gets easier.

When the crab is getting ready to shed, the pouch underneath begins to turn a dark blue or purple. The darker the color, the closer to shedding the crab is. This process is harder to spot on the males. The best test of a crab's readiness to shed involves grasping the crab by the back flippers and sliding the thumbs and first fingers out along the claws and holding them. When you have the claws, one with each hand, holding them by the first or outermost segment, take your thumbs and press outward and up on the hinged portion of the crab's pincher. As you increase pressure, there is a snap and the top part of the claw comes free.

If it is a good shedder, you can see the new claw forming under the old shell that has broken off. If you are too rough, the crab will drop the whole claw instantly when you snap the upper jaw. Most of the time I snapped the jaw hinge, just enough to disable it to make the crab easier to handle.

The crab will stop the shedding process if it is injured too badly, or just because it does not like the location of the shedder car it is being kept in.

We kept a couple of shedder cars. They were wooden barge-shaped boxes. They had small hole or wire mesh to allow for circulation, and were designed to float with the tops level with the water. The tops had a door held shut with wood button latches, which we opened to inspect and manage the crabs.

The bigger boxes were about two feet by three feet and about six or eight inches deep. These were mostly kept at the docks. The smaller boxes were the ones we would take out on the bay or along the creeks as we looked for crabs.

When the crab begins the shedding process, a dark line appears at the back of the shell. This becomes more pronounced as the shell opens up and the soft crab begins to emerge. At this point the crab is known as a "buster," as it is busting out of its shell.

Along the Forked River of my youth, the crabs were very predictable. The top of the tide was the only time to look for shedders and soft crabs. High tide was when they shed, whether on the creek, in the cars, or over at the sedge.

As I would go along the creek in my small garvey, I would use the crab net to propel the boat along the pilings and banks. Every so often, I would spot a crab hanging on and trying to hide. Sometimes it would be a doubler.

The blue claw will select a mate and carry her until she has shed and hardened up. He comes up behind her, and grasping her with his legs, he begins to swim about, and they go on what I like to think is the crabs' honeymoon. Together they are known as a "doubler."

The male crab will defend his wife vigorously, and becomes furious when caught while carrying. He will not only defend, but is highly aggressive and will downright come after you.

Crabs are cannibals. If you put a soft crab in with a big male, he will eat her. Sometimes I would catch a doubler and find the big male was eating the soft crab. Was that his wife or just some unlucky lady crab he'd happened to meet?

Soft crabs must be wrapped in wet seaweed and kept cool. This stops the shell from getting hard. Left in the water, the crab's shell begins to harden in about an hour. The shell at this point will buckle, and so one in that condition is called a "buckler."

▲   ▲   ▲

Crabs are temperature-sensitive — the colder the water gets, the slower they get. When the water cools in the fall, they begin to drop down off the flats where they were staying, into the deeper water. Here they are less exposed to storms and currents, and the water is warmer. In the spring they do just the opposite as the water warms — they go back up on the flats, and back up into the brackish creeks.

Crabs can communicate. It was well known among the baymen that if you went to work too early on the crabs, they would get up and walk away. Dad used to say you needed a little snow in the water before you went to work dredging crabs. Sometimes great gatherings of crabs would disappear, never to be seen again. Some baymen felt they left the bay altogether. That may have been true, as I have heard many times of fishermen in the ocean setting their nets on crabs. I think they must then spread the net out on the beach and let the crabs die, since they can foul a net so badly. After the crabs die they will fall off the net.

Sometimes the crabs that hadn't been seen for a while are found again. They might be a mile or more away in an area that had no crabs before.

How do they know to all leave at the same time? How do they all get to the same place? I have never read any studies on the subject, but I have a suggestion.

If you have a chance to be alone with a basket of crabs in a quiet place, you will notice a clicking sound they make. The warmer they are, the faster the noise comes. If they make a sound out of the water, it is reasonable to think they might make this sound under the water. Sound carries well underwater and a clicking sound may be how they tell each other what is going on. This sound might serve crabs to help locate the main body of crabs as it comes down off the flats, or serve as a distress signal when the dredges disturb them.

At a temperature of forty-two degrees, the crab will get up and walk. At temperatures colder than that, he will not move. Now, he has become a "dreamer." He will still try to bite, but he is moving in slow motion. It takes him awhile to recognize you, and if a cold wind is blowing, he is immobilized in seconds, and falls asleep on the deck in front of your eyes. He will lie there as long as it stays cold. If the sun comes out and it warms up, he will crawl away and jump overboard. If it is below freezing, you must get him out of the wind or he will die. The crab cannot take any freezing.

We carried a canvas to throw over the bushels; this would keep them until the temperature got down to about fifteen degrees.

Quite often we caught a mess of crabs while tonging in the wintertime. When I started raking I found myself catching more, sometimes as many as a bushel a day. That was as many as I could eat or give away.

▲ ▲ ▲

One particularly bad winter we were just about broke by the first day of January. I told Arlene I was heading south in my garvey and I wasn't going to stop till I found something to catch, if I had to go to the Delaware Bay.

I left Oyster Creek and started down the bay, trying the clams here and there as I went. When I got to where the channel runs south toward the Gunning Islands, I tried my rake in the channel. It was as I expected — no clams. What I did have was about seven or eight nice crabs in my shinnecock rake.

An idea formed in my head. I decided to try and catch crabs with my rake. I adjusted the sleds so they were only about an inch deep, and threw the rake back in the bay. I picked the drag anchor up and let the wind, which was blowing about twenty-five miles an hour, take me.

At first I didn't think it would work, then the rake started to feel heavy, and I could hear a light clicking as if there were some small clams in the rake. At last I decided to lift the rake. It was full of crabs!

I dumped them on the stern deck, and the cold wind calmed them down right away. I sorted them into my wire basket and ran the boat up to the bend in the channel by Gunning Island. My next drift down the channel netted me about two-and-one-half bushels of crabs. In a couple of hours I had about ten bushels on board.

Just then I looked up the channel and saw the watchmen, the enforcement agents of the Shellfish Council, coming along in their work boat.

This was bad, for I had a choice earlier that morning — whether to buy a clamming license or fuel for my boat. Times were hard; I bought gas and went to work.

I looked down at about fifty clams that I had caught.

I hated to do it, but I dumped them over the side. If I had no clams, they couldn't get me for clamming.

I had never heard of anyone catching ten bushels of crabs with a big rake, so there was no law against that. But if they decided to look in my boat, my new secret would be out of the bag. Not only would they know how I caught them, but where I found them, and crabs had been scarce that winter.

I let my drag anchor down and made believe I was hard at work raking clams, out in the gale of wind, as they approached. I gave them a great big, friendly wave. They waved back and kept on going. I was relieved, as they were notorious for getting people on the first day of the year.

I caught eighteen bushels of crabs that day, but because I was not prepared for crabs, I had no baskets to put them in. I had crabs a foot deep, all over the boat.

I didn't dare get in to the docks much before dark for fear of being found out. If the word got out, it would start a "gold rush," as we called it on the bay.

The next day the wind died down to about twenty miles an hour and I caught twelve more bushels of crabs.

I needed the wind to pull the rake through the bottom, but the weather report for the next day called for almost no wind. I knew if a crab dredger came by and hit those crabs, I would be watching him load the boat while I scraped for four or five bushels.

I had a big, strong friend, whose marina was shut down that time of year. I offered him a third if he wanted to pull the dredges the next day. He agreed.

We dredged the next day and caught thirty-eight bushels. We didn't come back in until dark to avoid giving ourselves away.

On the fourth day the weather warmed up and it started to rain. On top of that, seven boats showed up and started working on the crabs. We went home with twenty-eight bushels.

The fifth day the rain continued and the crabs were getting livelier as the bay warmed up. Now there were twenty boats working on our crab spot. Our catch for the day went down to about twenty bushels.

Day number six found the same number of boats looking for crabs, but the "gold rush" was over. The crabs had disappeared.

We did not find those crabs for about three weeks. They were about a half-mile down the channel from where we had first caught them. I developed a leaking head gasket and ran the boat up to Cedar Creek Marina for repairs.

▲　▲　▲

Crabs have a short life span. Around the end of January, or sooner if the winter is bad, anyone raking the bay will start to find dead crabs. As the winter wears on, the numbers of dead adult crabs increase until most of the crabs are dead. This happens regardless of the severity of the winter — their life span is over.

Raking in the spring, it was common to find crabs that the baymen had missed. It is somewhat depressing and sad to pull up rakefuls of big male crabs, all dead and all wasted.

An increasing number of crabs were also caught in crab traps. When I left the bay in 1987, commercial crabbing in the bays was limited to winter crabs. A small number of baymen were starting to set crab traps and sell crabs in the summer. Now I am told many people are setting traps up and down the bay — miles and miles of crab traps. It is another "gold rush" that is over-harvesting the resource. If we add commercial crabbing to the sport crabbing of the general population, enormous amounts of crabs are being taken from the water.

In the days before all this, the bayman often had good times catching the winter crabs. Sam Hunt will tell you about catching seventy or eighty bushels in a day. Catches of forty and fifty bushels were common during the Depression, one of the few times the bayman did better than many other people.

When we started working on the Cedar Run flats when I was a boy, the crabs swam by all day long. We caught all the crabs we wanted as we worked along. You could see them coming on a still morning. They swam right up on top of the water, their flippers breaking the surface. They seemed to like to go with the tide.

I suggested to Dad that the sedges should be full of crabs, but he said, "No; nobody knows where they go." This was completely different behavior than was exhibited by the crabs in Barnegat Bay, just a little further north.

In the early 1960s I knew an old waterman down on the Chesapeake Bay who told me a similar story. When I talked to him about soft crabs, he said they had lots of hard crabs in the area, but never caught soft crabs. Nobody knew where they went to shed.

Like the clam, the hard crab still survives, but the two share the problem that their numbers are greatly reduced.

chapter nine

The Scallop

*I am sure Dad and Edgar kept it
quiet for as long as they could, but the
word gets out, and more and more folks
got into the scallop business.*

I used to check out Dad's wire basket at night, because
he usually had something in it. It might be a flounder or a mess of crabs.
It might be an odd thing that he had caught out on the bay. One night
I saw the most curious shellfish in there.

They were a beautiful golden color, turning to white at the center of
the bottoms and on the outside edges. The top of the shell was clean
and tended more toward brown in color. The hinge area, which appeared to be the only straight line on the creature, sported two small
shell fins. Radiating out like the sun's rays from the hinge area were
ridges that grew larger as they neared the edge.

"What are they?" I asked. I thought I knew everything that grew in
the bay.

"Scallops," Dad replied. "We are catching a lot of them."

He said they were dredging crabs in the channel and when they
brought the boats around, they had to turn at the edge of the flats, and
that's where the scallops were. He had brought these home to eat.

We all gathered 'round as he showed us how to open and extract the meat from the shell. He selected one of Mom's paring knives with a flexible blade and inserted it into a small crack in the shell, just ahead of those small fins. He angled the knife up so it would cut close to the top of the shell, and with a rotating motion, opened the scallop.

He pointed to a large white muscle that he had exposed. "That is the only part you eat; the rest you throw away."

Coming in with the point of the knife to the base of the muscle, he lifted a girdle-like membrane with a flip, and the shell was clean. The white muscle stood ready to be cut free in one more movement of the knife. In fifteen minutes or so, he had a good mess opened up and took a break.

Mom floured and breaded them, and started frying them. The smell was intoxicating! They were the best things I had ever eaten out of the bay. I asked Dad why he didn't sell them.

"Scallops have been around a long time," he said, "Nobody has ever been able to sell more than a few bushels. They don't keep well, like clams do, and there is no market. What a shame."

One night my father had six or seven bushels of scallops shipped to New York with the trucker who ran the baymen's crabs to Fulton Fish Market in New York City. When I asked about it, he said he and Edgar Barkalow had talked it over and decided to send some to see what would happen.

The next evening, the buyers called them. They did not want more in the shell. They wanted them shucked, washed and cleaned, and placed in special gallon cans. They were then to be iced down and shipped in bushel baskets or fish boxes to the market.

Dad had an addition to the house well underway, and so one of the unfinished rooms became a shucking house. Edgar started shucking in his roadside clam stand, as I recall.

We all worked together as a family, and soon were moving a fair amount of scallops. I am sure Dad and Edgar kept it quiet for as long as they could, but the word gets out, and more and more folks got into the scallop business.

It was the start of a new era for the bayman. There were no laws covering the scallop; it had never had commercial status. But that soon ended. The state came up with rules and regulations for the small shucking houses that were springing up here and there. The Shellfish Council set the seasons and regulations for harvest.

For about thirty years after, we had a scallop industry. We went from a couple of baymen to a couple hundred boats working when there were any scallops to catch.

Those early years were wonderful. We would leave the docks at about seven a.m. on clear frosty mornings, and be back by ten-thirty or eleven a.m. with forty bushels. (Scallops, along with crabs, were the only species that were dredged on the part of the open bay bottom that was not leased. The mature creatures have short life spans and do not live through the winter. It is the young and immature that must be returned to the water if they are to reproduce.)

We would pull the dredge and it would be full of the most beautiful scallops. There was very little grass or dirt, as we called bottom debris. We culled out the small and juvenile scallops, throwing them back in the water. You want the biggest and best when you are shucking your own. It's worth the trouble to have a good grade of large scallops to handle, as time per bushel is shortened and product weight and quality is up.

Scallop season was to become a regular event. Come November, it was time to rig up and go scalloping. When I left to join the Marines in 1959, I left a clean bay that had some problems, but none that I thought were serious. I had much to learn. I joined the Marines the same year the biologists planted the grass over by Sedge Island. I would return home four years later to a different bay.

I couldn't believe my eyes that first scallop season back from the service. The boats were incredible — there were long, sleek skiffs from Keyport, fat cabin cruisers, outboards, bay garveys and rowboats. About 100 boats were plying the waters where there had been maybe twenty when I left.

Not all people saw the value of the scallop, and I knew that we had problems — problems caused by boaters from other walks of life who decided they wanted a piece of the action. When we hauled the shells from shucking to the Forked River dumps, I could see piles of scallop shells as high as my head. The sad thing was, mixed through and composing a goodly portion, were many small scallops, still alive. They were snapping their shells closed in an effort to move. The most pathetic of all were the baby scallops, hanging by their elastic-like umbilical cord from the shells of their uncles and aunts and moms and dads.

All the baymen I knew were enraged, but it seemed nothing could be done. Although minimum size regulations were put in place, I never heard of anyone being checked by enforcement. Anybody could catch scallops, and everybody did. A mess of fresh scallops could be had just by taking a walk along the bayfront. Some people were making a few dollars selling what they got there. But, all those boats!

There were plenty of scallops in those days, but you had to stay on them. The whole bay was not solid scallops. Concentrated areas of scallops were generally not too big, and the trick to a good day was to keep your boat and dredges where the scallops were.

Now, you get a gang of boats, all going around and trying to stay on the same spot, and you have the makings of a problem. Add in a little wind, and one or two skippers who don't know how to run their boat and you have a real circus.

What also surprised me was the location where we were catching the scallops. Where we caught before, Sedge Island and Clam Island flats, there were now no scallops. When I checked there with my dredges, I caught nothing but grass and tube worm masses. The baymen said the grass had come into the bay while I was away in the Marines.

It began to be easy for the bayman to see that the grass was affecting the scallop population. As the grass spread south, the scallops moved ahead of it. Each year the concentrations of scallops were another mile or more south. The scallops that took hold where there was grass were smaller and growing tube worm deposits on their shells.

The tube worm had existed only in one spot, over toward the inlet, in the channel. Now it began an advance to the south with the grass. It is a light-colored, coral-like growth that is found on submerged objects in the bay. Its growth can encumber the movement and life activities of the scallop. The scallop moves from place to place by opening and then closing its shell rapidly. This action also serves to feed the animal as it pumps the stirred-up sediment through its filtering system, extracting the matter that has food value.

Another interesting fact I learned about the scallop is that it is the only shellfish I knew of that had vision. It is sometimes called the blue-eyed scallop because of rudimentary blue eyes that are found around the inside edges of the shell.

Its trend of southward migration continued through the rest of its history until the shellfish had moved to Beach Haven — the tube worm and grass with it. At that point, having no more bay to move in, the scallops seem to have disappeared forever.

Around the mid-1960s, Edgar Barkalow lent me a study of scallops that had been done on Long Island, if I remember right. The study said that there are only two generations of scallops alive at any time.

This startling bit of information led me to examine our New Jersey scallops, and I came to the conclusion that this was basically correct for our scallops also.

If the study was right, then it would be very easy to visualize the bay scallop as extinct. As the life span of the animal is only two years, it would take only two years of unsuccessful spawning for the blue-eyed scallop to disappear from our bays.

▲ ▲ ▲

When Dad and Edgar started catching scallops, they used the same dredge or rake they had used for crabs. Dad had a welder and made his own dredges. Soon a new type of dredge with a cutting bar instead of teeth was being built in the back yard. The scallops were not in the bottom, but on top of the bottom. The cutting bar merely scraped them up, to be washed back into the basket or main body of the rake by the motion of the dredge through the water.

Most of the time we carried three scallop dredges, two that were worked from the stern, and one for a spare. Many days it took two men to keep the stern deck clear of scallops. The third rake wound up being pulled off the bow as a drag to help bring the boat around into the wind when conditions were bad.

Scallops have a rough, sharp edge where the new growth is occurring. We used cotton gloves through the season, as they provided the manual dexterity to sort out the catch. Some days we would wear out two pair, the catch would be so rough.

The first shock of cold water through the gloves seems unbearable. On a winter's morning, when the wind is blowing, our hands would quickly grow numb. As we worked, sorting out the catch and pulling the dredges, a wonderful thing happened. We began to feel the tingle of the returning heat to our hands and soon our hands felt perfectly warm. As long as we kept on working, our hands would stay warm, as would the rest of our bodies. Take a break for a sandwich and coffee, and you had to start all over again! We didn't break much on cold, windy days.

Dredging for scallops was like tonging for clams. You got real sore for the first couple of weeks, particularly the hands, from the constant pulling on the ropes as you hauled the dredges. Then you would get "broke in," and you would harden up to the work.

A bushel of scallops weighs about 60 pounds and must be handled, or lifted, eleven times:

1. It is lifted aboard the boat and dumped on the culling board.

2. The bushel is lifted from the culling board and thrown into a wire basket.

3. The full wire basket is dumped into large grass sacks.

4. The grass sack (woven from rough fiber) with the scallops inside, is carried up forward to keep the weight out of the stern.

5. The grass sack, with the scallops, is unloaded from the boat to the dock.

6. The sack is lifted from the dock and loaded into the truck.

7. The sack is unloaded from the truck and carried into the shucking house where it is dumped on the shucking table.

8. The scallop is picked up from the table and shucked. The remains are thrown into the trash.

9. The trash is carried out and dumped on the shell heap.

10. The shells are loaded into the truck.

11. The truck is unloaded at the landfill.

If each bushel weighs 60 pounds and we lift it eleven times, we have lifted the equivalent of 660 pounds. If we do the numbers, we can see that to process forty bushels of scallops, we must lift about 26,640 pounds of weight.

We must also consider the weight of the dredge, about 30 pounds, times the number of times it is pulled, about 100 in good conditions, to come up with another 3,000 pounds.

If we add another 50 percent for what we throw back, we can see that the bayman had to lift about 15,000 pounds to process forty bushels of scallops.

When you weren't catching, you were shucking. Sooner or later a shell would break, or you would stab yourself with the shucking knife. Hands that are immersed all day in the bay do not want to heal, and "saltwater poison" would rear its ugly head.

We were never quite sure what caused it. One day you would wake up with a small boil on your hand that would not heal despite attempts to care for it. It would get larger and more painful until it was about the size of half a lemon. It now was an abscess. The next stage began with a red line that started up your arm, and you had to go see the doctor. Dad had to get his lanced a few times, but mine responded to penicillin. Local folklore said that if the red line reached your heart you were a goner.

Another problem to be encountered in harvesting was that scallops, unlike clams, do not seal tightly and tend to lose a lot of body fluids. These fluids are very corrosive and eat up metal very fast. A new truck would rust out in two or three years.

Scalloping was a hard way but a good way for the bayman to take. As time went by, scallops vanished from the scene and baymen no longer go forth in the fall to harvest them. There is some question yet today whether the scallop is to be found at all in our bays — another species that is gone, perhaps forever.

Oystering

I felt so disgusted by my experience with the way the state had allowed the oyster industry in Barnegat Bay to be handled that I never became involved in the government-run oyster projects in South Jersey.

No one knows who he or she was, but one day thousands of years ago, the first human stepped out of the forest and onto the meadows of Barnegat Bay. The explorer was likely a member of a small group of hunter-gatherers whose ancestors had begun the migration many generations before.

Perhaps they walked along one of the many steams that flow out of the woodlands. The bird that they would later call the sea eagle startled them by diving into the water and catching a fish. This osprey flapped its great wings toward a huge nest, which they could see along the woods line.

The leader proclaimed that this was a good sign, and they moved on toward the great lake that they could see in the distance. The water crawled with crabs and sparkled with schools of bait fish. Wildlife abounded, for it was early spring.

If they were hungry there was food aplenty — ducks, birds, fish, deer, and rabbits.

What did they think of the oyster when they first saw it? Could they have guessed it was edible? Did they think the wrinkled, contorted shell to be a sign that it was not good to eat? Or did they think the oyster might be a close enough relative to shellfish found further inland?

Oysters grew from the larval stage by attaching themselves to large horse mussels that lived on the banks along the water's edge. Young oysters grew straight up from the live mussel, while the older oysters were lying down, their host mussel having died.

The discoverers of this new food, this new land, had come a long way. They might have built a fire to roast the fine ducks the hunters had shot. The children gathered some of the oysters and put them in the coals. Soon the shells opened and the smell of steamed oysters wafted in the air. The leader, still suspicious of the objects because of their odd looks, pulled one off the fire and sniffed. It was too tempting, and he took a tentative taste. It was good; the first oyster feast would begin.

▲ ▲ ▲

I used to catch, now and then, unusual rocks or stones from the bay in my rake.

How did they get there? I wondered. Did they fall off some barge years ago? If so, why just one lonely rock out here by itself?

Then I began to collect them. I kept them on the rails where I could see them and meditate over their origins as I worked.

One day as I worked along, I saw something. One of my rocks had a groove in it. Placing my fingers in the groove, as if they were a forked or split stick, I saw that the rock looked like a crude stone hammer or hatchet.

I remembered something from long ago. When we tonged oysters off Good Luck Point, we always knocked the spat (oyster seed) off the mature oysters and returned them to the water. Every once in a while, as I got tired toward the end of the day, I accidentally threw my spat hammer overboard instead of throwing the oyster in the bushel. So Dad would only give me a junk tool to use — old wrenches or a piece of iron. He knew I would throw it away sooner or later.

Now I began to see a new picture of the native American Indians I knew had been here. I had pictured them wading the flats or the creeks for oysters. Now I realized that when the old ones came to the shore in their yearly migrations, they had to bring all of the stone tools they would need, as Barnegat Bay has no natural stone in or around it.

Once they were here, they carved dugout canoes. Weather permitting, they went out on the bay for fish and shellfish — the earliest baymen. I could picture them on still days paddling out to the deep water over the sand edges where the biggest oysters grew.

The procedure would go something like this: They pushed a sharpened stake into the bottom to anchor the dugout. The best divers went over the side in search of oysters. Bringing them up, they threw them to their family in the dugouts. The others knocked off the spats to be returned to the water. They would take the extra effort to throw back the spats because they had respect for the Great Spirit and the fertility of the bay.

In every society, tools reach a point where they are no longer good for much, but are still too good to throw away. They are junk tools; if they are lost it is no big thing. This type is what they would have used to clean the spat off with — stone tools that would do the job, but were not the best.

I became convinced that these stones were lost in the bay by some of my long-ago ancestors.

Most of the stones were of a size and shape to fit my hand comfortably. There were some exceptions. Several times, I caught larger triangular rocks. These were about eighteen inches along a side and about three or four inches thick. All of them were flat on one side and concave on the other. They were worn smooth and had no sharp edges.

A stone of this size would take a lot of strength and energy to carry down to the shore. Once there, it would have many uses. A person could grind on it, use it as a table to work on oysters in the canoe; or, because it was three-cornered, use it as an anchor, as it would have been the best shape to tie a line on.

The shell piles that the Indians left along the shore are mute testimony to the value they placed on oysters as a food source, and to the oysters' availability before the coming of the white man.

Early writers tell us of the foods they ate while at the shore, and quite often oysters are mentioned. I have never read anything saying the shellfish were in short supply or the bay was depleted.

▲   ▲   ▲

The history I have heard begins with my grandfather June. In his youth he sailed out on Barnegat Bay for oysters. They oystered all the way to the head of the bay. The bay was full of oysters.

In those days, and in my youth, the Forked River flowed east, as all water does on coastal New Jersey. The Oyster Creek Nuclear Generating Station has had such a great need for water that it has consumed from the north branch, the middle branch, and the south branch of the creek. Needing still more water, it has drawn from the bay, causing the Forked River to run to the west at its mouth. The water used for plant operations is discharged into Oyster Creek.

The oral history of the oyster in the baymen's culture was unremarkable until about 1920. Then, according to the old men, a group of oystermen from South Jersey became politically powerful enough to wipe out the oyster industry in Barnegat Bay.

The first step was to lease the bay under the existing system that gave them legal ownership of whatever was on the bottom. Next, they brought boats and large dredges and went to work. They piled the oysters, spats and all, on big barges and towed them down to South Jersey.

It was said that when they were done, there was nothing left of any value; they had dredged the bottom clean.

When I asked, "Why didn't you do something?" the baymen answered, "We tried to. The crooked politicians had all the power. No one would listen to us. We had to watch as they robbed the bay of her oysters and us of our living."

Needless to say, there was much bitterness among the baymen of my grandfather's generation because of this.

No oysters were caught in the bay until 1959. The winter of '58-'59 found a good set of oysters off Good Luck Point and Toms River. I knew that there was some trouble on the bay, although I had not paid much attention. My focus was on getting out of school and onto the bay.

▲ ▲ ▲

We tonged oysters in much the same manner as we did clams. The difference was that oysters, unlike clams, lie on what we called the "top of the bottom." They only needed to be scraped up, not dug out as clams did.

Tongs surfacing full of oysters were shaken out with a clatter onto the rails. When the rails filled up, we stopped and cleaned them of spat and shells. Bushel baskets were waiting to be filled for shipment to market.

Now closer to the situation, I could see right off the bat that the mood of the baymen was foul. Gone was the good-natured bantering that was so common among them when they were making a dollar. They were grim-faced and surly, and I would soon find out why.

As I looked around on my first morning oystering, I could see that sticking out of a large expanse of the bay were cedar trees with the tops on. They were stakes marking leased plots. The area where we were working was less than a third the size of the leased area.

The next thing I saw was that all the boats on the leased areas were dredging. The mechanized teeth of the dredges worked in sharp contrast to the labors of the baymen, who were lifting a tongful at a time in the open areas.

I began to ask some questions.

"How come those fellers can dredge over there?" I asked.

"Because it's their oyster lot," Dad said.

"Did they put the oysters there?" I asked.

"No," he replied. "The good Lord put those oysters there, just as he did with ones we are catching now."

I was dumbfounded. How could such a thing be?

"How did they get those lots?" I asked.

"The Shellfish Council gave them the lots," he said. "We got wind of what was about to happen, and decided to go together to the next meeting to try to stop the leasing. When we got there that night, we were told that the meeting had been canceled. After the main body of baymen had left, the council members showed up and they had a meeting. When it was over, those men owned most of the oyster ground."

I wasn't a particularly motivated student in school, but I had absorbed enough to know that this sounded nothing like the government they had been telling me about.

"Now that it was done," he continued, "there seemed to be no undoing. Those in power seem to think we are outlaws and the men with leases are honest. The truth is the opposite. They plunder the bay and rob us all."

I chewed on that for awhile, and came up with what I thought was a solution that might make the best of a bad situation. I knew that oysters are raised on beds; cultivated is the word used to describe the operation. We couldn't change what had happened already, but maybe we could dump all our oyster seed on lots and raise them, if we had a lot.

When I put the idea to my father, he laid his tongs down and sat on the rail. "I tried to get a lot," he said, "but was told I could not be trusted, and so could not have a lot."

I was shocked. My father was the most honest man I knew. I had never known my father to break a law, any law.

I looked around the bay. The baymen who were working there — Edgar Barkalow, Bernie Penn, Frankie Penn — were all honest baymen.

"They don't have lots either, because they can't be trusted?" I asked.

"That's right," my father said.

It made no sense.

"Why can't they be trusted?" I asked.

"An honest man is greatly to be feared, especially by a dishonest man. For that reason this thing cannot be fixed. We must be content to accept what we cannot change," Dad answered.

Fixing me with that no-nonsense look of his, he said, "I want you to understand this. You didn't hear anything, and you didn't see anything. Do you understand?"

I knew what my answer had better be, but in my heart and soul I promised myself I would one day set the record straight; and those men who were responsible would regret robbing the bay and the baymen.

▲ ▲ ▲

Oysters are traditionally caught and sold only during the months containing the letter *R*. That April the oysters started to die. They turned milky-looking and ran out of their shells.

At first we blamed the dredgers, who having cleaned their lots off, were now slipping in and dredging the open ground. It started to look like war was about to be declared, guns and all.

It never happened. The oysters started to die, and shortly thereafter we had to leave to go clamming, for lack of live oysters to catch.

I went up the bay to look for oysters every year I worked on the bay after that. I was never to catch a live oyster off Good Luck Point again.

The baymen at the time blamed the oyster kill on the Ciba-Geigy plant at Toms River. This plant, which was starting up around that time, was licensed to empty a great many different chemicals into the bay. There was also an outfall pipe, which allowed them to discharge a larger amount of waste into the ocean.

It wasn't too much later that MSX, a virus that kills oysters, made its appearance in South Jersey and the Delaware Bay. I thought that perhaps the plant had been blamed unfairly and this virus had caused the oyster kill. I have in my possession tapes I made of a meeting between Rutgers University Professor Hal Haskin and the Commercial Fishermen's Council. I asked the professor about MSX and he said plainly that we never had MSX in Barnegat Bay.

What did kill the oysters? To some of us, the Ciba plant looked like the prime suspect. The good doctor blamed the loss of the oyster on the Manasquan Canal, saying the downstream flow had been destroyed by the water flow through the canal. I couldn't buy that, as I thought the canal was opened long before the oysters had been caught off Toms River and Good Luck Point in 1959.

If you look at old maps of the Jersey coast, you will see that the inlets were not always where they are now. In some cases where there used to be an inlet, there is no sign of one today. Cranberry Inlet off Toms River has appeared and disappeared in certain spots over the years.

The oyster is an organism that can tolerate a wide range of salinity. It can live by the inlets where the salinity is high. It can live up in the brackish water of creeks. The point is, we had oysters in the bay when we had an inlet off Toms River. If that didn't interrupt the downstream gradient, surely the Manasquan, or Point Pleasant Canal, as it is called, cannot be completely to blame for the loss of the oyster in Barnegat Bay.

At least once a year I decided to look up the bay for oysters. I tried to pick a nice day when I needed a break. I took tongs, a big rake, and a fishing pole. A setting pole, at least twelve feet long to feel the bottom, was also on the boat.

I would start looking just north of Cedar Creek. About a mile south of Good Luck Point I would catch my last clams — after that, nothing.

I would work all the way to Swan Point, south of the Mantoloking Bridge, before I caught anything alive again. All that way up the main channel, in the middle, on the edges — nothing alive. No oysters, clams, crabs, fish, seaweed, just miles of dead bottom.

At Swan Point I caught a clam one day. I worked on up to and into the Metedeconk River, which had a small triangle of open water showing on my condemned area chart. Once clear of the bridge I found a few oysters and clams — not enough to go all that way to work on, but enough to give me hope.

A short time later, one of the watchmen who policed the bay got me aside and told me I was on his lot when I went over into the Metedeconk. I asked him why it wasn't staked as required by law.

"I don't need to stake it," he replied. "Stay out of the Metedeconk."

I didn't see anything that was worth fighting over, and I had been doing a lot of that, as you will read later on. On the trip back I put the big rake away and laid the tongs across the decks for ready access as I tried the bottom on my way home.

There were places where the bottom was bare, and in some places there were huge piles of oyster shells. About a mile north of Cedar Creek I started to see a clam or two. All that bottom and nothing alive. At this point I put my gear away and headed home.

When I left the bay ten years ago, I knew where the sedge oysters grew. They grew on mussels, as the old men said, but not in Barnegat Bay.

I would catch an oyster now and then from the Manasquan to the black hole near Atlantic City, but not in Barnegat Bay.

I felt so disgusted by my experience with the way the state had allowed the oyster industry in Barnegat Bay to be handled that I never became involved in the government-run oyster projects in South Jersey.

I do not know what the answer is, and I don't want to believe there is none. I do know that a dead bay is not much of a legacy to leave to the future.

When a bay dies, the causes should be found, for the safety of all those who live on or around it.

chapter eleven

Other Shellfish and Marine Life

*The presence or absence of a species
in an environment says a lot about the
environment itself. The condition of that
particular subject tells us even more.*

One of the reasons for this book is to give testimony of
the life that once lived in our bays, and in particular, Barnegat Bay.

The presence or absence of a species in an environment says a lot
about the environment itself. The condition of that particular subject
tells us even more.

Some of these life forms were more important to the bayman than
others, but I suspect that all are of about the same importance to the
environment in their roles of maintaining a healthy ecology.

The following is a brief account of my experience with some of the
many other marine life and shellfish that were found in our bays. Many
are not seen in abundance, if at all, today.

Bluefish: This fish was a very common catch for the bayman. The bluefish of years ago were much easier to catch than they are now — of
course, there were more of them.

We used tarred hand lines with about six feet of wire leader and a
red-and-white-feathered jig. The tar preserved the lines, and the feath-

ered jig was all we needed to attract the blues. Trolling on the way home at night, we quite often caught one or two.

When the fish schooled up and we saw the birds working on them, we trolled around the outside of the school and had a good time catching the bounty.

One day when I was about sixteen, I was on my way home from Wrangle Point in the outboard garvey. I saw the birds working off Forked River and ran over to catch a couple fish. I caught ninety-eight bluefish in about an hour. They were about $1 \frac{1}{2}$ pounds, just right for eating. We put what we did not eat in the freezer.

In the oral history of the bluefish, it was said that in the old days they were so many, and so aggressive, that they actually drove the mossbunker out on the banks of the meadows.

Bloodworm: A marine worm, the bloodworm is used by fishermen for bait. They live in the mud of tidal flats.

Blowfish: A type of puffer, the blowfish was a common fish, but was not plentiful when I was young. In the sixties and seventies its population swelled to plague proportions, then in later years it became hard to find. I did not see one in the last ten years I worked on the bay.

Besides the hard clam, several other types of clams are found in our bays:

Soft clam: The soft clam, or "piss clam," as he is sometimes called, was at one time a commercially harvested shellfish in Barnegat Bay. During my years on the bay I never knew anyone to catch enough to sell, although I know my grandfather June and other baymen did in the early part of the century.

I discovered that many lagoons had good growths of soft clams in the banks that were left unbulkheaded, and in the winter I would steam a few. We always made sure to steam them well to kill any organisms, and we caught them where few, if any, houses had been built.

Razor clam: Perhaps razor clams are called that because of their resemblance to a straight razor. The razor clam is long and slim, the speed demon of the clam world.

We were out on the bay with the kids one day, and they brought me a razor clam they had found. We laid it on the bottom of the shallow water and the clam expelled water out of its siphon and shot a few inches away. It did this two or three times and rested for a second or two. Then it extended its tongue into the bottom and stood itself up on end. With a kind of pumping motion it quickly disappeared out of sight into the sand.

I was working off Rose Cove one morning when I noticed that the water was filled with some small swimming organisms that were too small for me to make out. I found a quart jar and scooped up some of the water from the bay to take a look. I estimated that there were about 200 small razor clams shooting around in that quart of water. For about two hours the tide carried a stream of razor clams by my boat; there must have been billions of them.

Mud clam: The mud clam is a small white-ish clam found in mud bottoms. It looks somewhat like a hard clam, but never gets much bigger than a littleneck. We never sold or ate them.

Blood clam: Sometimes called a hair clam, the blood clam is actually a cockle; at least I reached that conclusion from something I read. If you break one, its reddish interior looks a little like blood, hence the name blood clam.

There were also duck clams and a small black clam, neither of which got much bigger than a quarter of an inch long.

Conchs: In Barnegat Bay we caught only the smooth conch, which we sometimes called a winkle. They eat clams. I placed one in a basket of clams that was floating in an inner tube, and it didn't take long before he started to come part way out of his shell and engulf a nice-sized cherry.

In the lower bay, below Long Point, I began to find the pointed conch. These grew very large and were found intermixed with the smooth conch. These two animals exist wherever clams are found.

We pickled the conch, using only the white meat, which we first cut up and boiled. The smell of boiling conch was always a lot better than it actually tasted.

Somebody told Dad that the hound dog would like boiled conch and get fat on it. It was true. The hound dog got so fat he did not want to run rabbits anymore. We took him off his conch diet, but it did no good for that year. It was the following year before he got his ambition back and was any good for rabbit hunting.

I used to give my conchs to the Latorre family who ran the Cedar Creek Marina and they made an Italian sauce with conchs and tomatoes as its main ingredients. They always gave me a jar to take home.

Many kinds of crabs can be found in our bays other than the hard crab:

Calico crab: We caught one type — called a rock, calico, or stone crab — and ate it when it shed in the wintertime. We caught them soft, when the ice was on the bay. I enjoyed many a soft crab dinner in the middle of the winter when you would not think a soft crab could be found.

Spider crab: These crabs are found up and down the coast. They display some of the same behavior as the hard crab in that they double up. While soft crabbing with Pop in Bullinger's Cove, we caught a big male spider crab and his mate off the banks. On examination she showed the discolored purplish pouch, as a hard crab would exhibit.

Fiddler crab: This crab was not found in the Forked River area in my youth, perhaps as a result of the spraying of DDT to kill mosquitoes that was done by planes taking off from the Forked River airport. When we moved the boats to the causeway at Manahawkin, and later on to Cedar Run, there were millions of them out walking about when the tide was down. In my last ten years on the bay I never saw a fiddler crab, although some say they are reappearing on the banks of undeveloped meadows and marshes.

Hermit crab: Hermit crabs were found up and down the bay. This cute little crab makes its home in the shell of conchs and winkles of the right size. When he gets too big for his home, he finds another a little bigger and moves in.

There were other small crabs that had no name for the bayman; my favorite was the small crab that we would find in the oyster and sometimes in the scallop. They lived inside the shell with the host animal, and may have performed some service that we did not know about.

Drill: In my experience the drill is found about anywhere that shellfish are found. They rasp, or drill, a small round hole in the shell of their prey to gain access to the animal inside.

Eel: The eel is a snake-like fish that is a scavenger of the bays. He likes to eat things that have been on the bottom for a while.

Dad had an oak eel pot that my grandfather had made. It was about three feet long and tubular. About sixteen inches in diameter, it was cone-shaped on one end and open on the other. The oak strips were turned back inside on the smaller end, in a funnel design. The oak strips that made up the funnel were sharpened, so that once the eel had entered, he would find a barrier of sharp oak should he try to leave the trap.

I got the urge to have some fried eels one time, and I asked my dad about using the pot. Dad said he did not want any eels that had been eating dead horsefoot crabs, as it affected the taste. I asked about making up a bag of mosquito netting and placing the bait in this bag to keep the eels from eating. I suggested using conch for bait, and he said that under those conditions he might like a few.

I broke the shell off a couple of conchs and put them in the bag that I had made. I put the bag inside the eel pot and tied a burlap bag over the open end of the pot. I tied a line on the pot and lowered it over the side of my sixteen-foot garvey which was tied up by Dater Horner's houseboat in Forked River.

I checked it every day, and for four days, nothing. Dad said the pot needed to grow some algae on the wood; the eels would not use it if the wood was too fresh.

The fifth day when I went to lift the pot, I could barely get it in the boat, it was so heavy. The pot was full of eels. You could not get another eel in if you wanted to. I had about fifty pounds of eels and I only wanted a mess. I picked out the biggest. Unable to sell or even give away the rest, I dumped them back in the water.

Eels bed down into the bottom in the winter and can be caught with an eel spear. I tried a few times, but never had much luck.

Flounder: The winter flounder was a welcome addition to the baymen's diet. When we tonged in the winter, we hung a couple of lines from the stern cleat for flounder. These lines had very small hooks and were baited with a little piece of clam. The bait was small to encourage the flounder to swallow the bait and hook whole. We kept an eye on the lines as we worked, and seeing the line moving, we laid the tongs down and pulled the fish in.

Some of the baymen set flounder fykes (long, bag-shaped nets held open by hoops) and did well at it. When I asked my dad about it, "There are too many in it now," he said, "and you run the risk of losing your fyke nets in the ice when the bay freezes over."

Fluke: The fluke of summer does look a lot like the winter flounder, but they are two different fishes. The fluke grows much bigger and has a different taste altogether. The fluke is a more aggressive fish and requires different techniques to catch him. Some baymen caught and sold fluke, but the fluke was never a serious commercial item for the baymen.

Grunt: The grunt was a small (about six inches), silvery fish. I used to catch a lot of them when I was a boy. They made a grunting sound when caught. The fish was gone from the bays by the time I was a young man.

Horseshoe crab: The "horsefoot," as he was called on the bay, is a very ancient creature more closely related to spiders than crabs. It is found all over our bays, but likes a high level of salinity. It is not eaten; it was used for bait. For another purpose, the big females were opened up and the eggs fed to poultry.

They mate in the spring to early summer. At this time of year they assemble together in large numbers for their mating ritual, which can be observed on the full moon. One of the best places to see this was the bank from Long Point north to West Creek.

At least three types of mussels are found in Barnegat and her sister bays:

Brown mussel: When I was on the bay, a brown mussel could be found growing on any bayfront marshland. I asked my dad about eating them, and he got a thoughtful look and said, "I don't think those are good to eat, and I think that is why we don't eat them." He seemed to have the impression that they would make you sick.

Blue mussel: The blue or black mussel — its name depended on whom you were talking to — is delicious to eat. Found more toward the inlets and on the flats, the blue mussel is not nearly as common as it once was. Barnegat had a huge set of mussels each year that I worked the bay. They always die off when they reach about three-quarters of an inch long.

Horse mussel: It was a point with most of the old men: They knew that the brown mussel was not the same as the horse mussel. The horse mussel was bigger and the horse mussel was the mussel that the sedge oyster grew on.

Oyster cracker: The oyster cracker is a fish with a big mouth and small, evenly spaced teeth. It grows up to twelve to fourteen inches long. He has a rather unattractive body and is mostly all head. They hide under and within submerged objects. They love old cans and wide-necked bottles. I think they hide inside and wait for dinner to swim by. They didn't spend much time cracking oysters, as our bay had none.

Perch: When my younger brother, Dave, was small, he was the most avid fisherman I ever saw. He would fish for hours any place that he thought might have a fish. One day he came home with a fish I didn't know. He said he had caught it at Stout's Creek in an area where some lagoons had been dredged, a couple years after the work had stopped. The next day I walked out through the woods to Stout's Creek with him. We had a lot of fun and caught seventy-eight perch that day. We brought them all home and they were cleaned and frozen for the winter to come.

These fish were in brackish water not far from the edge of the woods. I have also caught them in the bay, and I think they can be found anyplace in between.

Perch are a school fish and where you catch one, you will most likely catch more. Sometimes a move of fifty feet or less will start you catching fish; you have to find them. Some baymen made a few dollars catching perch through the ice on the Mullica River.

Ray: The stingray is found on our flats, particularly near the inlets. The flats around Sedge Island in Barnegat Bay and the flats from West Sedge to Hester Sedge in Little Egg Harbor Bay are good places to look for them.

I had heard many times that rays were good to eat. One day we took a small harpoon and went drifting across the flats looking for a ray to spear. I soon spotted one lying on the bottom and harpooned him in what I hoped would be a vital area.

The ray took off in a hurry, towing the boat along behind. After a couple of runs, it expired quickly and we were able to haul it on board. It was about three feet across and weighed about thirty-five or forty pounds. We cleaned and iced it down and went on home for our supper.

Breaded and fried, it was one of the worst meals I ever had. The ray is not to my liking. It has a stringy and somehow primitive taste. I never harpooned any more stingrays.

Sea bass: Sometimes called "little black sea bass" by the baymen. The sea bass grows about eight to ten inches long and resembles the tautog in looks.

This was one of the fish I caught when I was very small. Some days I caught as many as a half-bushel of these fish. I did not see, catch, or hear of a sea bass in my last twenty years on the bay.

Seahorse: The seahorse was common when I was a boy, but over the years its numbers slowly declined. I can't remember seeing any the last years I worked on the bay. They are about three inches tall and look somewhat like a marine horse with a curled tail, which grasps the vegetation.

Sea robin: If you go fishing and you catch anything at all, it will probably be a sea robin. They have rather large fins on the side, a big mouth, and are brownish-to-orange in color. I am told that some people eat them. I never wanted to try.

Sharks: Grandpop June had a story that he told about sharks. It seems that he and a couple of other men were scratch raking clams over by the sedge. The baymen at that time used sneakboxes to put their clams in as they worked. One of the men felt something bump into him as he worked. Thinking it was the sneakbox drifting into him, he bumped back without looking around. Feeling another stronger bump, he looked.

Grandpop said he "never saw such a leap as that man made" getting

into his sneakbox. It was an enormous shark, which had come up behind him as he worked.

I saw sharks many times over the years. I ate the sand sharks we caught
along the channels and they tasted like soft crab to me. The skin is rough
as sandpaper and requires a sharp knife to cut.

In the mid-fifties when we were working out of Mud City and Ship
Bottom at the foot of the causeway bridge in Manahawkin Bay, I noticed
some boats that were going around towing lines with what looked like
inner tubes fastened between the boat and the line. "What are they doing?" I asked my Dad.

"They are fishing for sharks," he said. It seemed there had been an
incident with a shark, and people were trying to catch him.

I have had treaders tell me sharks had hit them, but it is uncommon
in our bays.

Art McNemer said that a school of sharks attacked him one day down
by Barrel Island. The men were in shallow water and saw the sharks
coming in. They got in the boat, and the sharks began to hit the boat
and bite the outboard motor, which they tilted up out of the water. The
baymen poled the boat to a nearby island, the sharks hitting the boat
and biting the pole as they went. They got on the island and the sharks
hung around for some time before they could go home. It is rare, but it
is possible to be attacked by sharks in our bays.

The shark is very fast in the water.

There is a kind of duck-like bird that we called the helldiver, really a
grebe, which molts in the winter. Because of this, it is nearly flightless
and if it does not dive it will go skittering away across the bay surface at
a high rate of speed.

I was running in to the mouth of Oyster Creek one evening when I
saw what I thought were two helldivers racing along on top of the water.
A closer look revealed that what I was really seeing were the fins of two
sharks that were slicing through the water.

The shark does not seem to mind low salinity and at times will go well
up into streams and lagoons. Sightings of sharks in the Forked River of
my youth were not unheard of, though I never saw one there.

The shark was never a commercial resource to the bayman.

Striped bass: I mentioned earlier that the striper had been an important resource to the bayman but, with the passing of laws against netting in the bays, it became a thing of the past.

I did have a fishing pole, however, and I will tell you how I caught my first stripers. I had hit something and bent my propeller. I could still run the boat, but only at low speeds. The clams were up and I decided to take my time for a week or so and catch what I could while the catching was good. When the clams went down, I made repairs.

I was chugging home one night when I noticed the gulls working by the banks; "bird play," we called it. I ran the boat in closer to the banks and I could see the tails of some big fish breaking in close to the shore.

I anchored my garvey up on the meadow and walked along the shoreline to where the fish were. I had a light rod with a spinning reel and two or three blue and white Rebel lures, about four inches long.

I started casting and soon had a nice striper, about five pounds in weight, lying on the meadow grass. I caught about a half-dozen in about twenty minutes and I was hooked on the striped bass.

I had seen bird play along the banks before, but I was in too big a hurry to pay attention. When you go too fast, you miss a lot. Slow down in your boat, and you will see and learn more.

Stomatapod: I caught a strange creature one day that seemed to be a cross between a shrimp and a lobster. I took it home, but had no alcohol to preserve it in, so I put it in my freezer. A few days later I got some alcohol and put the animal in a large jar with the alcohol. My son Tom and I had done some work for Mike Kennish and the Barnegat Bay Research Project, so I gave it to Mike.

He told me later that it was a stomatapod. It was the only one I ever heard of or saw in my years on the bay.

Shrimp: Now and then I would catch a big shrimp in my tongs or rake, and I felt for some time that there might be more. But, how to find out? I knew that Bernie Penn and others caught grass shrimp over by the sedge, and I decided to make some shrimp nets.

I built the nets and combs and started looking. The nets worked over by the sedge and I looked for about a month, all the way down to Barrel Island in Little Egg Harbor. I found lots of grass shrimp, but never caught one large shrimp in the nets. If they are there, I could not find them.

Tautog: Resembling the sea bass but growing much bigger, the tautog is not scaled as the sea bass is, but must be skinned. A delicious fish to eat, he is worth the work.

Now and then in the winter I would catch a crab pot that had been lost and was lying there on the bottom. It would invariably have tautog in it. Once I caught a trap that had about fifty pounds of fish in it, all tautog. How they survived inside a crab trap was beyond me. They seemed to be in good shape. I saved a couple of the big ones to eat if I felt in the mood; otherwise, I just let them go.

"Zebra fish": When I was a young boy sitting and fishing off my father's boat, a school of fish would come around, swimming about a foot under the water. When I asked what they were, my father said he did not know, but they were found over around Mud Channel and the sedges. They had broad black and white stripes like a zebra, and so I called them zebra fish. They would not take my bait and I never caught one. They have gone from the bay, and I have not seen one since I was a child.

There were so many more small fishes and other creatures that I cannot describe or remember them all. When I was trawling around the bays looking for shrimp, I was amazed by the diversity of marine life that entered my nets. I think that scheduled inventories and cataloging of the marine life in our bays might be a good idea. It would serve as an environmental indicator and point out what needs to be done in the years to come.

I am encouraged by recent reports that the bay waters have appeared cleaner, at least to the naked eye. I am also told that the fishing is better. This is a good sign that we are on the right track to improving our environmental quality.

chapter twelve

The Meadows

I would find old boats that had been left there in bygone years. Some were far afield, near the woods, and I knew some great storm had carried them there, too far back from the bay to ever be recovered.

The meadows, or tidelands, are vital to the life of our bays. When we think about the environmental health of our waters, we must take the tidelands into account. The bays are not just big holes filled with salt water. They call on the marshes and meadows to sustain all phases of life, and the two are interwoven ecological systems.

Organisms that live in the bay depend on the marshes for food that the tides deliver to the bay. Some organisms spend their youth in the marshland ponds and creeks. There they find protection from predators, until they are of an age and size to assume life out in the bays, or in some cases, the ocean. Tidal marsh is extremely well suited as a feeding and breeding ground for many birds, mammals and crustaceans. Reptiles and amphibians abound, and the marsh teems with unique vegetation.

The soil is highly organic, so much so that in some areas it will burn. When I was young, we would sometimes dig the peat, as we called it, and use it for heating fuel for the winter. We could see where others had worked the same area. I have never read of this being done in New

Jersey, and know of no other account of using the peat from our meadows as heat.

The meadows played a large role in the survival of the bayman. Oral tradition has it that the meadows were used for salt works (as in the case of one of my ancestors), for the grazing of cattle, the cutting of salt hay, and for market and pleasure hunting. The meadows were ripe with beach plums and bayberries for anyone who wanted them.

Market gunning was gone by the time I was young. It was, however, still fresh in the minds of the old men who talked about it. I do not think it took place on the scale of Michener's *Chesapeake,* but it was at one time not unusual for men to take a big gun, or a small cannon, and shoot ducks in mass, after dark, out on the meadows. They talked about the AT&T ponds by the wireless station at Forked River as the ones most often shot over.

I can recall seeing cattle grazing on the meadows around Bayville as a boy. In other areas, all that was left to show for that activity were now and again a fence post sticking up out of the meadows.

Salt hay was still being cut when I left the bay. Because of its salt content it was useful around the homestead in the winter. We used it to protect new concrete when there was a danger of freezing.

The first time I can remember being on the meadows, they were flooded. Dad had set some decoys out off Stout's Point, and had anchored the boat down the banks a ways. He got his gun in one hand, and I climbed off the boat and onto his shoulders as he stood in the water.

Off he walked through the water to a spot where the ground was higher, where he had built a small duck blind. I was amazed that he could do this with his bad leg. I still can see the view of the flooded meadows from my father's back.

As I grew older I learned to shoot, and I ate the ducks and occasional rabbits that I found there. Deer were there, though I never shot one on the meadows. I used to see them sometimes when I ran the boat in to count off in the lee, out of the wind. They seemed to like the cool breeze off the bay in the summer.

The meadows were a great place for a young fellow to explore. I would find old boats that had been left there in bygone years. Some were far afield, near the woods, and I knew some great storm had carried them there, too far back from the bay to ever be recovered.

The bayshore itself might yield any treasure; all the cast-up floatables of our society were to be found there. Once, standing on the bayshore, I saw a large animal go swimming by. I am quite sure it was a manatee, though I have no idea what he was doing in Barnegat Bay. The water was about three or four feet deep along the bank, and it passed within ten feet of me. I could see it clearly. It was not a seal; I was used to seeing them over by Barnegat Inlet while crabbing. One certain seal used to like to sit on a small island off the north point of Forked River. The island is gone now, as is the seal.

It has been about a half-century since I started to go out on the bay with my father. Back in the early days, the only house you could see from the bay off Forked River was a small building that was a part of the AT&T wireless station. It was shut down and vacant.

You were alone on the bay, except for an occasional boat. The essential wildness was there. The meadows, for the most part, were intact. Now if you go out on this section, you will see a wall of houses. The meadows are becoming more and more built up. In spite of all the lip service that we pay to environmental concerns, it is obvious that money still opens doors — and gets a new house built on the meadows or bayfront.

When there was one house on the meadows, the effect on the bay did not amount to much.

Build five thousand houses and the damage is five thousand times as great. We know without a doubt that this is so, yet, as a people, we allow it to go on. We pass laws and regulations with plenty of loopholes so the next guy with some money can still get his dream home with a view of the water.

Meanwhile, we complain about pollution, population, taxes and traffic. Perhaps it is time to reassess our situation. We might come to the conclusion that we have gone too far already.

To use one of my crude analogies: If you operate on a person and take out one of his lungs, he will live — not as well as before, but he will live. If you take out the other lung, he will die. If the meadows are to the bay as lungs are to a person, we have already taken one lung out and are working on the second.

What will happen when the bay can no longer breathe? What will we tell our grandchildren about the stink hole that the bay will become if we build on the meadows without concern for anything but the almighty dollar?

East Lacey Road in Forked River runs fairly straight east from Route 9 until it makes a bend and straightens out and heads for the Captain's Inn and the township docks, which are not far. As you come around the bend, you will notice that the road is quite high above the water in the creek, and a marina now stands there. When I was a small boy this area was called Hebeler's Dock. My grandfather, my father, and other relatives tied their boats there. In those days there was a gravel slope and a beach, with a single tree growing about halfway up the slope to the road. A great storm came, and the men took me along as they cared for their boats. The tide began to rise, and so did the talk of losing their boats. When the creek reached a certain point, they waded to the boats and strung lines to the tree. The tree wound up anchoring three or four boats, as still the water came higher.

I was there with Dad in the car when the wind shifted off and came around to the west. The tide at that point was about three feet from the road. When I go there today and look at the height of the water in relation to buildings new in the last fifty years, I am convinced that the shore area will, at some time in the future, experience major disaster.

What bothers me is that Grandpop did not think it was too bad of a storm, and made no bones about having seen worse.

The old people did not build on the marshes, as they thought it was not a healthy place to live and because they thought a storm would come and blow away whatever they might build. Only time will tell the rest of the story.

I have read that Barnegat Bay has been around for ten thousand years. It is so sad, what we have done to it in the last fifty years. If we are to save the bays, we must realize that we must save the tidelands also.

chapter thirteen

Boat Design:
Evolution of the Garvey

The outboard motor was almost nonexistent in those days. It was regarded as a cranky, hard-to-start joke.

The 16-foot garvey, right, and the 24-footer on the frozen bay in December, 1960.

In the beginning, when men had a heavy load to get across the bay, they built a barge. A barge is little more than the next step up from a raft. Its drawbacks are that it is large, square-ended, and hard to move through the water.

It was part of the oral history of the bay that a man named Garvey put a motor in one of those barges and the first garvey came into existence. Later sources told me that this man's name was Jarvis Pharo, and the local men called him Jarvey, or Garvey.

I heard around the bay that early garveys were also sailed. I only saw one under sail in all the years that I worked on the water. I was working on my boat one day down at Burton's in West Creek when a garvey, about eighteen or twenty foot, came sailing out of the creek. She was rigged like a catboat, with the mast well forward. The wind was not too good, and, watching her having quite a time working her way out the channel, I thought of what my father had said.

"The days of sail are over," he told me. "It just takes too long to get where you are going."

As Mr. Garvey chugged along in his motor-driven barge, he must have known that he had a good idea. I wonder how long it took before another barge showed up that ran across the bay faster or smoother.

The garvey evolved in different ways in different areas. A bayman could spot a Barnegat garvey from a Parkertown boat as easily as telling night from day.

Many years ago, my father-in-law, Roy Martin, who was a Merchant Marine, left a book on seamanship at our house while he was away at sea. In it was a description of two types of hulls, a displacement hull, which travels through the water, and a planing hull, which skims over the water.

The first motorized barge was a displacement hull. It traveled through the water without much regard to its design, other than to stay afloat. Its earlier, motorless counterpart would have moved along with the help of cedar poles or a sail; now the motor pushed it faster. Some hydrodynamic changes were needed.

Sloping the front downward toward the back of the boat would lower the boat's resistance to passage through the water. So would making the barge narrower, and sloping the stern.

"Bringing the bottom lines up," or "cutting the stern up" was a well-known method of making sailing boats and rowboats. It allows the displacement hull to move through the water easier.

Nature provided the original blueprint for hulls to glide through the water. Ducks and other waterfowl have displacement hulls — they are swept up in the stern.

Although Mr. Garvey is remembered over time, the first man to plane out one of these garvey boats is forgotten. I like to picture him running his new barge out the creek. He reaches down and pulls the throttle wide open. For the first time ever, a barge rises up and runs on top of the water. He must have been surprised. How about the rest of the men? Perhaps they had never seen a rooster tail in the water before. It would not take long before other men were building similar garveys and the boat had a planing hull.

The first bayman who built a tunnel in his boat — to raise the propeller up and allow him to go across shallow water — is lost to history. In Barnegat Bay, we had tunnels long before they began building them into commercial boats. The development of the tunnel was the result of the particular environmental conditions of the bay.

The Barnegat Bay garvey in general, was the largest and highest in freeboard of all the area work garveys along the Jersey coast. The long reaches of fairly deep water in a rough bay generated the need for high garveys. The water is shallow, or shoal, from Long Beach Island out to about a third of the distance across the bay; then it deepens. Incidentally, the rise and fall of the tides in parts of Barnegat Bay is only a matter of inches, compared to the tides in other bays, which often have several feet of tidal difference between high and low tide.

A bow cabin was also an identifying characteristic of the boats from Barnegat Bay. The bay develops big, wet waves when conditions are right. The bow cabin was designed to turn water from the boat. A windshield that folded down was common, and helped stop the spray from coming aboard.

As we migrated down the bay in my youth, I noticed that the boats I saw began to change. When we worked out of Mud City and Ship Bottom, most of the boats were small. Mud City boasted a few small garveys about fourteen or sixteen feet that had small air-cooled motors in them. They were miniature inboard garveys. They were sometimes worked out of, but most often the local boys were to be seen putting about and having a good time in general.

When we moved the boats to Cedar Run, it was easy to see the difference in the boats that were assembled there. Alongside the boats from the upper bay, as we called Barnegat, the boats from the lower bay were narrow and low. Tow garveys were common there, and they tended to follow the same design — long, low and narrow.

The outboard motor was almost nonexistent in those days. It was regarded as a cranky, hard-to-start joke. Now and then you might see one bolted on the back of a pole garvey, as tow garveys were called in the lower bay. Most of the time it didn't move much.

These pole garveys were cut up in the stern like a rowboat or a sailboat. It was common in years gone by for a bayman to pole out the shallow creek and out on the bay. He would work until he had his day's pay, and then pole the boat back up the creek at night.

Unlike Barnegat, the bay off Cedar Run is shallow. It is mostly flats, all the way across to Long Beach Island. This is the type of bay where a small garvey that a man could push with a cedar pole would evolve. The powerboats would not need to be high and beamy, because a shallow-water bay does not get as rough as a deep-water bay.

The flats off Cedar Run were rich spawning grounds for clams in those days, and men came from many areas to work. I began to get an education from the boats I saw. The men from Parkertown were mostly in very low, narrow boats. The boats from Tuckerton were similar, except that they nearly all had stern cabins, or houses. Some of the Tuckerton boats had nice V-bottom designs. They were somewhat different from the Barnegat V, in that the Tuckerton boats used a parallel curve for the V. This resulted in a V-shaped bow. As time went by, I was able to see both types of V-bottom boats built in both areas.

▲　▲　▲

I am not sure when Mr. Garvey put his motor in his boat, but the motor dates him. Even more, the motor dates the evolution of the garvey along the Jersey shore.

In the early 1950s all work boats had motors that came out of a car or a truck. If someone had a marine engine in his work boat, I do not remember it, and it would have been a most remarkable thing. The motors that I saw were mostly older motors that came out of old or wrecked vehicles. I am certain that this was the case from the start. The early garveys were powered by motors that would have been easy to get, and that the boat owner would know how to work on.

The problem was that the early motors were not as powerful or as well designed as today's engines. The drilled crankshaft took a while to develop. Until then, motors had oil pressure to the main bearings only. The rod bearings were lubricated by a dip system. As the crankshaft turned, a small cup on the end of the connecting rod dipped into the crankcase oil. This, occurring at high speed, forced a small amount of oil into the rod bearing, lubricating it.

To work, this system depended on the motor being fairly level. The motor could not be mounted at shaft angle or it would burn out for lack of oil to the front bearings. A universal joint was installed to overcome this problem. A universal will not take the thrust generated by the propeller, and a thrust bearing was installed. This was the way all motors were found to be installed in work boats in the beginning.

Most of the motors that wound up in work boats got there only after they had proven themselves by wearing out once in a car. My dad always rebuilt the motor out of an automobile he had worn out. He liked six-cylinder Dodges and Plymouth engines. They were flathead design, with a drilled crankshaft. The basic block remained unchanged from 1942 until 1959. This meant that parts were easy to come by.

So, the development of the garvey was tied to the automobile engine, with the corresponding time lag that it took for the motor to work its way into a garvey.

Early car engines were not that powerful. I seem to recall that the Model A Ford had about twenty-eight or twenty-nine horsepower. In the forties, seventy or eighty horses was a lot. I saw a couple of boats that had straight-eight cylinder engines. These were great hunks of iron. They were so heavy that anything gained in power was lost trying to keep all that weight on plane.

It was the fifties that would bring major changes to the garvey. Around 1950, General Motors put out an overhead valve V-8 engine with a drilled crankshaft. This allowed for oil pressure to the rod bearings also. By the mid-fifties, the big three auto makers were all producing powerful V-8 motors, and some of them started showing up in the baymen's boats.

The introduction of epoxy fiberglass technology into area boat building enabled boat makers to build a stronger boat capable of handling this extra power.

The outboard industry was starting to produce a better motor with more power. This was to bring about more design changes, as the outboard became more popular on the bay. The sixteen-foot garvey that Dad built in the mid-fifties was different from any small boat that I had seen to that point. It was not cut up in the stern, as a normal tow garvey would have been. Instead, it was made like an inboard flat-bottom boat. In fact, she looked like one. She had a nice rise to the bow, a good amount of beam, well forward, and the pinched stern that makes the lines of a garvey so pleasing to the eye.

With the addition of a 7 $^1/_2$ horsepower outboard from Sears and Roebuck, she was complete. She would plane out and leave a rooster tail in the spring when she was light. The motor was dependable and the boat was well liked. A fellow from the beach asked Dad if he could take her measurements, as he was going to build some rental boats and liked her form. Dad said, "Sure," and in a couple of years I started to see more and more small garveys that looked like ours.

I don't know about other towns, but Barnegat had a tradition where the baymen got together and raced their workboats on the Fourth of July. As time went by, a new class of garveys began to develop. They were called racing garveys.

An association was formed, and rules were developed for the different classes. The last I knew, they were making speeds of about 100 miles per hour. As Dad used to say, "If you put enough power on a barn door, it will go!"

If someone had stored one of the boats from those days and decided to put it in the water today, it would not be allowed to run. By today's standards, the motor would be considered too dangerous to operate. The original manifold was used, and the exhaust portion ran hot. Most engine boxes of the time had a panel that could be opened up to allow air in to cool and prevent fire.

There were no flame arresters on the carburetor, and there were no special starters or generators that prevent sparks and explosions. Gas tanks were made of any container that would hold gas. That could be a five-gallon can or a beer keg, water tank, or gas tank from a truck.

Some of the boats used a car or truck transmission, with a coupling to connect it to the propeller shaft. Others were direct drive and were pushed out of the boat stall and started, having no neutral and no reverse.

I recall the story about one fellow with this type of rig. He shoved his boat out in the creek, and fired the motor up. The boat took off, and he started out the creek. The motor ran for two or three minutes and then it died out. It did not take too long to find out that someone had stolen his gas tank during the night. The motor was running on the gas left in the carburetor.

Some of the boats did not even have a water pump to cool the engine. They used what we called a Parkertown rig. This consisted of a pipe and fittings that were installed in the water flow from the propeller. When the boat was underway, water pressure from the prop wash forced cooling water through the motor. Of course, the boat had to be underway to run the motor long, or it would overheat.

The motors themselves were bolted to the stringers of the boat, usually with lag bolts. Some used only big spikes, driven through the home-made motor mount. They were humorously referred to as self-adjusting motor mounts. When power was applied to the engine, it tended to move into alignment, and smooth out the vibrations that come with an out-of-line engine.

In spite of these many violations of today's rules and regulations, no one that I can think of ever blew up, burned up or sank because of the motor or its installation. This is not to say that today's rules are out of place. The boats we are talking about were very open. The modern systems of today are much more enclosed. Gas tanks are under the floor, or in enclosed spaces, and the likelihood of explosions from trapped fumes is much greater.

If Barnegat had big, beefy garveys, Tuckerton had long, slim, fast boats. As the years went by, a merging of the styles produced some garveys that had steps built into the hulls. Art McNemer had a step garvey when I first knew him in the sixties. What made his boat different was the deep V found forward, and in the stepped portion of the hull. It had a 312 Ford, and was completely fiberglassed.

I saw boats in the Forked River area that had steps, and one that had sponsons like a hydroplane; all of these boats were quite speedy.

As the power of the outboard motor increased, the tow garvey became a speedster. Some of these boats were fast and graceful, while others were downright ugly. Of course, beauty is in the eye of the beholder.

I am sad to say that it looks as if the garvey has come to the end of its development. The cedar needed to build this kind of boat is only found in limited quantities today, and if you do find it, is very expensive.

The boats that were built in bygone years are disappearing as fastenings give out and the cost of upkeep goes up. When you see an old-time garvey, you are looking at a little bit of the past.

chapter fourteen

Dad Builds a Garvey

The boat was built almost entirely from plans that my father had in his head. This, in general, was how most of the Barnegat Bay garveys were built.

Merce, Sr. and Dave in the 24-foot garvey.

Our hound dog had run a rabbit into a pile of slabs down by Harry Gray's old sawmill, behind Murray Grove in Lanoka Harbor. I tried to call him off, but he didn't want to quit, so I went after him. I got to looking around and saw a set of garvey sides stacked up there.

When lumber was cut to build the sides of a garvey, the bark was left on the edges. When the builder went to work, he trimmed or edged the boards to suit the plans he had.

The year was 1957; I was fifteen and wanted my own boat. I went home and told Dad about the sides. He wasn't interested in building me a boat, but he was interested in building a new boat for himself. We took a ride over to Harry's, and he said he would sell the sides for thirty-five dollars.

When we got to the sawmill a day or two later to pick up the sides, I was surprised to find two or three trucks and several men standing around the edge of the swamp. They were listening to a bear growling and snarling down in the tangle of growth. Harry said the bear came every year about this time. He thought the creature was in a bee tree eating the honey. The bees were stinging him and that was why he was making so much noise.

I had seen bear tracks in the Forked River Mountains and I had seen his sign in the woods where I hunted. He had torn up large patches of ground in search of whatever it was he was eating.

We stood at the sawmill listening for a while and then we loaded up the sides, along with some other cedar that Harry had cut, and went on home. I wanted to see the bear, but they wouldn't let me go into the swamp.

When we got home, Dad and I put the cedar up into the attic to season and dry completely. There it would remain until the spring when Dad was ready to build the boat.

▲　▲　▲

When the weather turned nice, we went to work. We dug eight postholes in the ground, so that we had two rows of holes about 10 feet apart. The postholes in each line were about 5 feet apart. Once this was done, we placed a post in each hole and packed the dirt around them until they were solid and would not move.

Using a line and a level, we nailed a 2 by 6 across the 10-foot span between each pair of posts. When we were finished, we had a level platform on which the new boat would be built.

The next chore was to bring the garvey sides down from the attic and lay them out on the platform. Using a chalk line, Dad marked the bark edges and cut them off, so that each board had straight edges and could be fit together. He then placed them together so he had two rough sides laid out on the 2 by 6 crosspieces.

Next, he took a Skil saw and ran it down the seam where the boards came together. This got rid of any irregularities in the fit, and created a good tight seam that would swell shut.

The sides were then marked for battens every 12 inches. The battens were of $1\,^1/_2$ inch cedar. About 4 inches wide, they are used to strengthen the sides and tie the sides together. Garvey sides are like tong handles in that they have a left and a right side. Once you determined which would be what, you could begin to nail your battens on.

The battens were fastened on with eight-penny galvanized nails. The nails were left with 1 inch showing through the batten, to be cinched over at the proper time.

Using a thin piece of cedar that would bend easily, Dad laid out the curve for the bow. When this was done, he cut the first side. Next, we placed the cut side on the uncut side, and using it as a pattern, we cut and scribed the second side. Now Dad had two sides that were the same in size, height, curve and length.

When this was done, a form was built, about $8\,^1/_2$ feet on the bottom and around 9 feet on top. This was extra wide for the length of the boat we were building. The sides were about 24 feet long and would give us a boat about 23 feet when the sides were sprung.

A common formula for boat building is, figure about $^1/_3$ the length of the boat for the beam, or the distance across the widest point of a boat. For her length, this was the widest boat I had ever seen.

Next, using some of the common cedar lumber we had gotten from Harry, Dad built the stern. It was about 6 foot by 28 or 30 inches, and also had battens applied. When this was done, we stood the sides on edge, bottom side up, and fastened the stern corners. Then it was time to set the form.

First, Dad measured from the stern to where he wanted the widest part of the boat to be. The form was inserted between the two sides at this point and fastened with about $^1/_8$ inch of nail left showing.

Next, we took a measurement from one corner to the mark on the opposite side. This was compared to the same measurement from the other side. The sides were adjusted back and forth until the two measurements agreed. Dad called this "squaring the boat." Although it is hard to think of a boat as being square in any sense, in this way a boat is square.

Now the sides were braced and secured so they could not move, and corner braces were applied to the stern. We were ready to spring the sides.

Dad had several pipe clamps which he used to begin drawing the two sides together. At first it was easy, but as the tension increased, the wood began to snap and complain. At this point we gave it a rest and took a break.

Now was a good time to put some restraining cable around the bow section that was being sprung. If the clamps should slip, we wouldn't lose it, or be injured by the tension release as the side straightened out.

This done, Dad went back to clamping the sides and drawing the sides in to form the bow. The whole process took a couple of days. In the final stages he used burlap bags and boiling water to help steam the wood into its final shape.

He cut more 1 $1/2$ inch cedar, about 5 inches, and fit and fastened pieces between the battens all along the bottom. He called these pieces "grub pieces."

Next, double 2 by 10s were installed, running from the stern to the form. The bottom of the form was a 2 by 10 also. He nailed them in with sixteen-penny galvanized nails, and placed them on centers that would allow the motor to mount on them when the boat was finished.

Dad had wanted to build a V-bottomed boat, and had started to bend a piece of white oak. It resisted the boiling water and burlap bags. He jacked an old truck up on it, and still it would not bend. He kerfed the wood (cut a notch or groove in it) and steamed it some more — no luck.

He bought some 2 by 12s and cut sweep (a curve) for the bow from them. After they were installed, he was ready to start planking the bottom.

Dad started from the stern. He installed the planking widthwise across the boat, rather than lengthwise as is common with a skiff. There was much planing of the planking and the hull to get the bottom into its final shape.

Galvanized nails were set about $1/2$ inch deep with a nail set.

When the bottom was on, all nail holes were filled with a caulking compound and any seams that were not tight were also caulked.

At this point the whole family joined in, and we all sanded together to give the hull a nice smooth finish. The bottom was painted with copper paint, for its anti-fouling properties that helped keep barnacles and marine growth from forming.

▲ ▲ ▲

It was time to turn the new boat over. Dad removed the nails from the 2 by 6s and posts on one side of the boat only. He took the posts out of the ground, leaving the boat resting on an angle. About a dozen old tires were placed where the boat would fall. Some of my uncles showed up for the occasion.

The men all got together on the high side of the boat and began to lift. Higher and higher the boat went, until it was standing on its side. There was a hurried check to make sure the tires were in the right place, and the boat was let go. The men all jumped back at the last minute.

It hit the tires with a crash and bounced nearly off the ground.

Everyone walked around the boat and admired it. There was much talking and laughing. It was a good time.

In the next round of work, the boat must be jacked up and blocked like a proper boat. All the nails that show through the battens must be cinched over. This is a two-man operation. They are set with a nail set from the outside, and bent over and backed with a heavy maul by the person inside. This produces a good tight cinch job that will not work loose.

The main supports that run across the boat, Dad called deck carlings. A cedar block, the width of the rail, was applied to each batten. The decks themselves were of cedar strips that were ripped about $1 1/2$ inches wide.

The boards that wrap around the inside of the boat, Dad called combing boards. They were about 8 inches wide and were doubled, so that he had a combing about 2 inches thick. This combing board stood about 3 inches higher than the decks.

The clam rail went on the outside of the stern decks and the side rails. It was made of cedar strips about 1 $1/2$ inches by 1 inch. They were nailed one on top of the other until a 3-inch rail was constructed.

Around the outside, where the decks meet the sides, an oak rub rail was installed. It was there to take the wear if the boat should knock against something, a piling in a storm, for example.

The stern cleats, bow cleat, and the bow chock were also made of oak. Dad cut them out on the band saw, and carved and sanded them until they were smooth and ready to go to work.

The floor and the cross members that supported it were also of 1 $1/2$ inch cedar. The floor was designed so it could be removed in sections, in case of a leak or other problems we might have.

I think Dad had a friend with a boom on his truck come in and set the motor in the boat. It was a 1949 Plymouth flathead six-cylinder, and had about ninety horsepower. Dad set it up so it was direct drive, with a clutch. The boat would have a neutral gear, but no reverse.

The shaft log, shaft, propeller and rudder were installed. Much lining up of parts, drilling, shiming and bolting went on until one day, we were done. The boat had been painted and made ready in every way. The gas tank had been installed and the motor started.

One day, the local man who hauled boats showed up and loaded the boat on a trailer. We got in the truck and followed it down to Hebeler's Dock in Forked River. He backed the trailer in the water and the boat floated off.

It was a good-looking boat and showed only a trace of water as the new cedar started to swell. Within two or three days it stopped even that small leak, and was a tight boat for the rest of her life.

With the wide beam, she made about twenty-five miles an hour, which was considered fast for the times. It was a very stable boat, which is a feature of wide-beamed boats, along with the ability to carry large loads for their size.

The boat was built almost entirely from plans that my father had in his head. This, in general, was how most of the Barnegat Bay garveys were built.

Ice on the Bay

Nothing can stop it. I have watched it tear down concrete buildings and smash docks and pilings into splinters.

Clearing ice from the channel at Liberty Harbor in Waretown.

Sometimes ice would help the bayman by cutting clams out of the bottom, or scraping the scallops on the flats into windrows in its passing, but most of the time it was bad news.

"One winter the ice was thick on the bay," my grandfather June said, "and a northeaster with a big tide came along. The tide came over the meadows and drove the ice ashore. It drove the ice all the way across the meadows and cut down trees at the wood line."

As a boy I can remember seeing the scarred and bent-over trees the

127

storm left. Here and there, where the meadows met the woods, I found the proof of the event that my grandfather had related to me.

Ice that is only a quarter-inch thick can be broken easily. You can poke a hole in it with your finger. It has very little vertical strength. This same ice will sink an unprotected boat. Ice does have a lot of horizontal strength, and it increases as the ice gets thicker.

Ice is, after all, the frozen form of a substance that is already heavy. Water is very heavy — 8.337 pounds per gallon, to be exact.

Because water expands as it freezes, it floats.

Combining these two factors, moving ice is a juggernaut in slow motion. It is irresistible. Nothing can stop it. I have watched it tear down concrete buildings and smash docks and pilings into splinters. The piles of broken ice left along the bayshore could reach ten feet high.

Ice is grasping; it will lock around a piling and when the tide rises, so will the piling, dock, or whatever the ice has gotten hold of.

Preparing for the coming of ice was a fact of fall. As winter approached and the nights got colder, the skim ice would start to form on the water where we tied up.

It signaled the time to reinforce the boat with a winter coat of tin. Dad would haul the boat out wherever we were docked. He bought galvanized sheet metal in four-by-eight-foot sheets, and we cut it into two-foot strips. We used roofing nails to nail it on the boat.

When we were done, the garvey was sheathed in metal all along the waterline where the ice would make contact.

Some baymen would fasten oak boards along the waterline, but that was not the preferred method, as the ice would cut oak boards almost as well as it would cedar.

The best method until fiberglass came along was to sheath the boat permanently with sheet copper. It was an expensive way to go, and I only knew of one boat that was done that way. That boat belonged to Edgar Barkalow.

We kept a watch out for deeper winter, until one morning we would go to work and the water around the docks and harbor would be frozen over with ice about a quarter-inch thick. This was called windowpane ice.

Dad used to say that this ice was worse than thick ice. The boat will ride up on thick ice and break it down with its weight, but with windowpane ice you must push forward and contend with its horizontal strength, which is very strong.

One year, the owner of a certain marina was late with fall haul-outs. I watched as he ran a wooden skiff about a hundred yards to the travel-lift, through the windowpane ice. By the time he got to the lift, the boat was sinking. The sharp edges and the horizontal pressure of the windowpane ice had gashed the wedged-shaped hull.

Tin, copper, oak, it didn't matter. As the winter intensified and the ice got thicker, the morning would come when the bay was frozen over. It now had a "lid" on it, as we would say, and no one would go out through it; the risk was too great. The metal sheathing was easily torn off by heavy ice.

Fiberglass was new to the bay, but Dad tried it out in 1958 when he built his last boat. It worked great, and I went to a great deal of trouble to do my garvey right. I wanted to be able to work as long as it was possible before shutting down for the winter.

Now that the ice was making (forming on exposed surfaces), the routine in the morning was different. Even if you had freshwater cooling systems, which most of us did not, you had to drain the saltwater from the system. And in the morning, you had to reconnect your hoses and pumps and clear any ice from the systems or the motor would not cool, and you would run the risk of burning out the pump impellers.

Once this was done, the motor was started and run in gear. Then wash from the propeller would clear a hole in the ice behind the boat. The boat could then be backed out of the stall and turned enough to start out of the harbor or creek.

As a boat entered the ice, the operator felt a grinding, along with a sharp trembling and shaking of the hull. The harder the ice, the more severe was its struggle. The boat began to rise up and fall down as the ice below it broke down.

If the ice was very heavy and had not been broken in a while, we used to get three or four men in the bow of the boat doing the ice breaking. The added weight helped break the ice down after the boat had run up on it.

All the time we were doing this, a sharp eye had to be kept on the engine temperature, for the ice could clog the cooling system with the small pieces that tended to get drawn in. In later years we learned to use a brass strainer over the intake scoop, but the ice could rip this off, too, and care still had to be exercised.

One morning I saw Russell Horner, Sr. run his unprotected boat through the ice on a plane. Running on a plane means the boat is running on top of the water, instead of through the water at slower speeds. The ice was thin, but still capable of doing serious damage. When I asked him about it, he said he had discovered that planing out through the ice did less damage than running slow. When I checked his boat out, I could see that this apparently was so.

One morning I had gotten out into an open hole off Waretown, and was looking across the ice to the Game Farm beach where I wanted to work. It was a long way through the ice and I decided to try running on a plane to get there. The ice was about an inch thick. The boat planed out and we were on our way. The boat trembled and shook. The motor roared and the noise of the boat grinding the ice was nerve-racking. After about a mile of this, I stopped to check the condition of the fiberglass on the boat. It was fine, no sign of damage.

When I got to the area where I wanted to be, I broke a strip of water open over the clam spot and went to work.

By afternoon I had a good day's pay on board. The wind started to blow, and the ice moved a little with it. Looking down the bay, I could see more ice coming before the gathering wind. I wasn't too worried, for I had run in there on a plane and felt sure I could leave the same way.

When the approaching ice made contact with the ice floe I was working in, the whole mass started to move. The ice began to slide up on the Game Farm beach, and I knew it was time to get out of there.

I put my gear away and started out. At first everything was fine. The boat planed out and we did great until I got to the area where the new ice had moved in. The ice from down the bay was heavier, and had slid under the ice that I had been working in.

When the boat hit the ice, it could no longer plane and I had to slow down and break ice in a more conventional fashion. Now I had about three inches of ice instead of the inch I had broken on my way in.

Looking at some ranges, or reference points, on the mainland told me that I was in trouble. The ice was moving faster than I thought. It was drifting toward shore faster than I was running through it. Even though it seemed I was making progress, I was really losing ground and in danger of being put on shore, boat and all, by the drifting mass.

It was one time I was really glad for the big, powerful motor in the boat. I gave her all the power I thought she could stand, and checked my ranges. This time, to my relief, I was making some headway.

It took some time, but I cleared the ice pack and made it back to Waretown, a much wiser man about ice. If the ice had been thicker, I would have lost, and my boat would have wound up on the meadows. The same thing would have happened if the boat and motor had not been in good shape.

I know of baymen who lost their boats in the ice; the hulls cut and mangled by the stresses created trying to run and work in the ice.

The hazard was not just out on the open water. Once the bay has frozen solid, the boats must still be cared for on a daily basis. We used chain saws and shovels or whatever was on hand to break the ice around the boat. If this was not done, the pressure of the ice could do great damage to the hull and possibly sink the boat.

One very cold winter, the bay had frozen over and I had taken a job laying hardwood floors in Beach Haven West. It snowed every other day for about a week. I was not too worried about my boat; after all it was completely covered with fiberglass. I stopped by on my way home at night and shoveled the snow out of the boat, but I did not have time to cut the ice around the hull.

I was very surprised to find her "bow up" one night as I stopped by for my daily check. Getting aboard, I found that the exhaust pipe, which was about six inches above the waterline, was under water. I should say under ice, for it was so cold, no water could be found.

The ice had locked around the boat and held it firm.

Each time it snowed, the added weight pushed the ice-locked boat a little deeper. Because the snow that I had shoveled out was piled around the boat, I had not seen this until it was time to do something about it.

I went home and got our son Tom to help. We used whatever we could find to cut and break the ice around the boat. We worked till about eleven that night, before the boat, with a great lurch, broke free and assumed the proper floating position.

I never allowed the ice to get such a hold on my boat again. It was not worth the risk to the boat, or the strain on body and nerves, as we worked to undo the situation I had gotten into by not breaking the ice around the boat on a regular basis.

▲　▲　▲

It might surprise some people to know that ice on the bay is composed of fresh water. It tastes no different than ice on a lake. When salt water freezes, the salt is excluded.

However, salt ice, which is ice that has formed over salt water, is treacherous around the edges. Where the sun hits along banks and bulkheads the ice gets rotten. It may look just fine, and it can be a foot thick around your boat, but around the edges it will rot and you can wind up in the water if you are not careful.

I had a small garvey tied up at Beach Haven one winter, and Tom and I were down checking our boats. The day was foul and windy, and the temperature was around fifteen degrees. There was a hole in the ice, over in the channel just outside the marina where we were tied up.

I thought we might drag one of the boats out on the ice and push it to the hole where we might make a few dollars.

I walked around the boat on the ice and decided that the boat was a little too heavy for us to manage.

When freshwater ice breaks, you hear and feel it. Saltwater ice, particularly around the bulkheads, gives you no warning. One second I was on firm ice, the next I was going down through the ice and into the freezing cold water.

Dad had said, "If you walk on the ice around the boat, make sure you can grab a tie line or something, in case the ice breaks."

I caught a tie line as I went, and managed to stop my progress, when

I was in about to my waist. It was the only time I ever went through the ice, and I never want to do it again.

The truck was only about forty feet from the boat, but by the time I had pulled myself out and made it there, I was freezing. The wind cut like a knife. Tom got the truck started, and I got my boots off.

By now the cold had made me numb from the waist down. The old truck didn't have much of a heater in it, and I thought I would freeze to death before we got to Waretown. I did wind up with a cold that lasted about three weeks.

We used to make a few dollars taking up clams through the ice. It was another dangerous way to work. We would cut holes in the ice and use tongs or rakes to take the clams up.

Once clams are out of the water, they must be covered to keep them from freezing. As soon as we could, we hauled them to the waiting truck, where we covered them until we took them to the clam house.

Care had to be exercised that we did not fall in, because to come up under the ice would be fatal. Even so, there were other ways to get hurt doing this kind of work.

I recall one cold day, our son Tom drove a splinter about three inches long through his finger. It ended work for him that day, and it was weeks before his hand healed.

Sooner or later the winter would break and one day the ice would leave the bay proper. The creeks and docks would stay frozen for a while longer, and we would start trying to break the boats out so we could go to work.

This was one of the worst times for the boat. The ice might still be more than a foot thick. Those big chunks under the boat would hit the propeller as we tried to break out. Even if you had a heavy-duty wheel, as we called the propeller, you still most likely would bend or damage it, not to mention damage the rest of the boat from the heavy ice.

Ice on the bay meant hard times for the baymen. We never made much money when things were frozen up. We did work hard, just to keep the boat floating and ready to go to work when the weather finally warmed up. I am glad I am retired and no longer have to do this sort of work in the wintertime.

chapter sixteen

Clam Transplant Programs

*The boys and I sat there looking at
the largest gathering of men and boats
we ever were to see.*

Merce in his garvey during the Tuckerton transplant program.

Over the years that I worked on the bay, I became involved
in several interesting clam transplant programs. They were designed to uti-
lize stocks in marginal waters, either by harvesting when the water was pure,
or by placing the shellfish in the bay to cleanse themselves.

▲ ▲ ▲

Art McNemer and I were tied up at Norman Larsen's in Cedar Run.
We were talking one morning. "Are you going down to the Golden Thoroughfare?" he asked.

"The what?"

He began to tell me about the Bonita Tideway that flows by Brigantine. The state had opened a section of the tideway for clamming about
a year before. This was part of a program to harvest marginal waters

during the cold weather, when the waters are much cleaner.

Art said the clams were so thick you could fill your rake with a couple of short pulls. The baymen who knew about it and got involved had done so well that they started calling it the "Golden Thoroughfare."

An air of excitement began to circulate around the docks as some of us started to think about going. Some said it was a waste of time and money, but several of us wanted to give it a try.

We decided we would all run our boats down at the same time. If somebody were to break down, he could be taken under tow. None of us had new boats or motors, and I guessed we would have about a forty-mile run before we tied up at Brigantine.

On the appointed morning, we all showed up and started getting ready for the trip. We held a short conference and decided that Paul Lafferty, who was the oldest and the only one of us who had ever been down there before, would take the lead and set the pace. The rest of us would fall in as we left the docks.

By the time our ragged little convoy had left the tethers of the docks behind us, a cold, chilly southeast wind was starting to blow. It was really starting to kick up as we rounded Long Point. Three boats in our party of seven were outboard garveys, about sixteen to eighteen feet long. They steeled themselves against the wind and water as we beat our way down the coast.

Our planned route had been inland all the way. I was surprised when Paul turned his boat on a course that would take us out Beach Haven Inlet. I knew he had experience in these waters, and I stayed in line.

It was to be one of the roughest rides I ever had as we transited from bay to ocean. Our decks were all awash with seawater as we plunged and pitched our way out Beach Haven Inlet. I recall looking on as young Norman Larsen stood his boat on her ends. Why it did not go over, I will never know. The wind must have been blowing thirty to thirty-five miles per hour and seas were running about six to eight feet in the inlet.

An acquaintance of mine had been pestering me to take him clamming. He wanted to go to work on the bay. I had invited him along on what had looked like a nice ride down the coast. With the first big sea, he disappeared into the cabin. Now he popped out as the ride settled down once we were in the ocean. He looked like an owl that was getting wise real fast.

Somebody must have called the authorities and told them that a bunch of crazy baymen had gone out on the ocean on this wild and windy day, for a helicopter showed up and began circling about.

And so we proceeded on down to what we called Breakers Inlet, where we had a much easier time getting back in to sheltered water for the next leg.

Nobody sank; nobody broke down. We were lucky, and happy to run in the channels the rest of the way to Brigantine, where we tied up at a marina and drove home in the car my wife had brought. The young man who was my companion for the trip never asked to go out on the water with me again. He and his family moved inland about 400 miles not long after.

Clamming was to start at eight a.m. the next day. Four in the morning found me up, along with our young son Tom and his friend Jon Foreman, who were getting 10 percent for counting the clams.

We were at the marina by daylight, and it was a scene of frantic activity. Men were trying to get their gear on board and were starting up their motors. We took our time getting ready. We were about two hours early as it was. Meanwhile, a steady stream of boats was running out to the grounds. Most of them were concentrated in the southern area, but there were a number who rushed off to different sections, and I wondered how they knew where the clams were, considering this had been a closed area for some time.

We idled out at about seven-thirty a.m., and I anchored up just outside the main body of boats and shut down the engine. The boys and I sat there looking at the largest gathering of men and boats we ever were to see.

A couple of minutes to eight they all picked up their rakes or tongs and stood waiting. The marine police blew a whistle, and with a tremendous splash that plunged into that calm, still morning, work on the Golden Thoroughfare was commenced.

I dropped my tongs over and made a grab. The bottom was like iron;

there were lots of clams in it, but wasn't any good for my shinnecock rake. I picked up and started looking for some soft bottom. When I felt the bottom drop off, I realized that much of the thoroughfare had been dredged and was very deep. The bottom in these areas was soft, with few clams and much grass and dirt.

Coming up on the edge of the channel, I caught a rakefull of small clams, and quickly got the boat anchored up — bow and stern — so that she could not move.

I have never seen the equal of it in my life! The clams were so thick that all you had to do was throw the rake in and shake it a couple of times. It would fill to the top with 'necks and immature clams.

The boys started counting and bagging, and I kept on dumping clams. Tom and Jon could not keep up and the clams soon were piled all over the boat. When quitting time came, I had a small dilemma on my hands. I ran the boat in by the bulkheads for protection from the winds and we all counted for another two hours until we had separated all the legal-sized clams and counted and bagged them. I still had about ten bushels of clams that were too small to catch legally.

I was not willing to take a chance on getting hassled over the size, and we took a shovel and overboard they went.

I sold 9,700, and I estimate I dumped about 15,000 to 20,000 clams that were too small to sell. I think I caught about 25,000 to 30,000 clams that day. It was the best day I ever had, as far as the numbers go.

I worked down there for about two weeks until the catch dropped off to the point where I would be better off at home. I packed up. I was worn out from the hours and travel, and I have no memory of the ride home.

▲ ▲ ▲

The Tuckerton transplant in the late 1970s was the next program that I was involved in. It was different in that we caught the clams and then transported them out to temporary lots where they would stay until they had cleaned themselves out and were ready to sell.

(Clams are filter feeders. As they filter their food from the water, they can also ingest harmful substances such as coliform bacteria. This was determined to be the source of a hepatitis outbreak in the sixties when

I was away in the Marines. As the clams sit in clean water, however, they will in time clean themselves out as the water is pumped through their systems.)

Our son Tom had his own boat by now, and we showed up that first day along with a gang of other men who were all there for the transplant. It was most unusual in that the clams were all well up into the Tuckerton Creek, and we caught most of them where there were docks with cedar trees growing nearby.

This was very far inland to find clams in such numbers. They were all big clams and from the size, I would say they had been there for some time.

I stayed for only one day, as the area where the clams were was small and the number of boats large. As a result, by the end of the first day we had just about wiped them out.

I caught around 8,000 clams and hauled them out to my temporary lot. I drove a small stake in the water and dumped them all on the same spot. Once this was done, I took care to note the ranges and pulled the stake out.

When the appointed time came, I returned and caught back all but a few hundred. After that one day, I never returned to the lot.

The Manasquan transplant program was much different from the Tuckerton transplant. I left Waretown one morning and ran the boat up to the Metedeconk River. I tied up at a marina not far from the southern end of the Point Pleasant Canal. The next morning I made my way through the canal to the Manasquan River, where an area had been approved for the transplanting of clams.

I caught around 4,000 the first day and close to that the second day. I found pretty much the normal bottom-dwellers with the exception of a few oysters that were growing there.

By the end of the first day, my hands had started to burn. When I mentioned it to other baymen who where working there; I found they were having the same reaction. The water seemed to be acid or caustic. By the end of the second day, my hands were so sore I was wearing gloves. We were never told what might have been in the water that made our hands burn.

My boat was in good shape, but the ride through the canal at night was a pain in the butt. The tide runs with great force through the canal at times, and makes for a hairy passage in a loaded boat or one that does not have enough power. The relay lots were off Swan Point at the head of the bay, and so we came back through the canal with loaded boats at night.

The second day that I worked, I became convinced that the cream had been taken off the top. I would be better off working the bay back home and getting my day's pay at night. That was the disadvantage of working on a transplant program if the clams were not abundant — they had to stay on the lot until they were certified as clean by the state. Until then, no pay for expenses or time. I went back to Waretown with my boat and worked the commons while I waited.

As I recall, at this point in my life I was no longer involved in the politics of the bay, having withdrawn from such matters.

▲ ▲ ▲

One day I had gone to the Forked River flea market in search of some small thing that I needed. Arlene and the kids had gone along for a diversion.

The girls came to me with a puppy in their arms. "Look at the beautiful puppy, Dad," they cried. "Can we keep her?"

It was a beautiful dog. She was about six weeks old and had one blue eye. "What is it?" I asked.

"It's half Labrador and half Siberian husky," they told me.

I had just finished reading Michener's *Chesapeake,* and I was interested in a Lab for its ability as a boat and gunning dog. I wasn't sure that I wanted to take on the husky, although I thought it would make for a hardy and strong dog. Arlene said we could keep it, if I cared for it. That meant that the dog would go on the boat with me from the start.

This gave me another problem. Some baymen seemed to always have their dog with them and were never hassled. Other baymen were told they could not have a dog on board. Since I had never had a dog as a companion on the bay, I was not sure in which group I belonged. I decided to be brave, and we had a dog.

After the appointed time had passed, I got a phone call that on a certain date the lots off Swan Point would be opened for retrieving the clams. My source was part of a system that we had set up, and I had complete confidence in the man.

The crack of dawn on the appointed day found me making my way out Oyster Creek in Waretown. The wind was out of the northeast, ten to fifteen miles an hour and the barometer was falling. The weatherman was saying that we were going to get a good northeaster.

I ran the boat along the edges of the flats, where it was not too rough, and in about an hour I was up off Swan Point.

I could see a couple of other boats working on their clams. I went to work and found my clams without much problem. I anchored the boat with two heavy anchors off the stern to keep her from slatting about in the rising wind. I had dumped the clams all in one pile, and around one o'clock I had about 5,000 on board.

The wind had continued to rise and was now blowing twenty-five to thirty miles an hour. The smaller boats had gotten blown off the lots and gone home. All my papers were in order as was my boat. I was not too worried when I saw the watchmen coming. Except for the puppy, which was sleeping in the pilothouse, I knew I was legal.

They brought their boat around and hollered as to whether or not my anchors would hold them also. I replied that they would, and they threw me a line and I made them fast to my boat.

"What are you doing here?" they asked.

"I am taking my clams up," I said. "So-and-so called, and said the lots were open today, and here I am."

"You're not supposed to be here today," they told me. "It's tomorrow that the lots are open. You are in big trouble, Ridgway."

I replied, "There were other boats out here this morning. Where were you? If tomorrow is the day, why did they think it was today? My information is good."

Now they got angry. "Wait here," they told me.

I was a little curious where they thought I might go, out there in that gale of wind. I got credit for a lot of things I never did, but walking on the water was not one of them. I sat down on the rail while I awaited the outcome of their radio calls and discussion, which they were undertaking in the enclosed cabin of their boat.

Sitting out in the wind and not moving, I started to get cold. The hell with this, I thought, walking back and sitting down in my pilothouse. As soon as I closed the door, here they came, waving me back out of my house. They wanted this or that paper, which they had seen already.

The puppy, which had been sleeping, began to let out a howl now and then; she seemed to sense that something was wrong. Twice I saw the watchman cock his head and listen, but the noise of the wind and waves, along with the crying of the sea gulls, was drowning her out.

It was a serious charge they had made against me. If it were true, I could lose my boat, my clams, and my living. I reminded myself that my source was good, and I began to see a pattern in their behavior. Each time I tried to get out of the wind, they called me back out. Now they were not working on the radio. They were reading magazines and laughing.

I thought about the time someone took a gun and blew a hole in the bottom of one of their boats. I thought it was a bad idea at the time; now I wasn't so sure. I remembered the time someone put a live skunk in the cabin of the patrol boat. Was this the same boat? Did the house still smell like skunk? For sure, it still had a couple of skunks in it.

As I sat out there in that raw wind, I promised myself I would write about them. At last they came out of the cabin. "Well, Ridgway, you're wrong, but we are going to let you go this time," they told me.

"Thank you very much," I said. I quickly cast their line off and set them adrift. I asked the Great Spirit to please not let their motor start and to put them on the banks before I could help, but they got started and left, and I was glad of that.

I had lost a good hour, but I went back to work and caught a couple thousand more clams. When I counted off, I had nearly the clams I estimated to be on the lot and I headed for home, never to return to Swan Point.

By now the wind was blowing nearly forty miles an hour and it was taking the tops off the waves in the higher gusts. I had more than 7,000 clams aboard.

To fight the gale as little as possible on the way home, I stayed on the east side of the bay. I didn't run across the bay until I got to Forked River. That was the worst of the ride. I had plenty of power in the boat, and we just skimmed home after that.

As soon as I got home, I made a few phone calls. I was right. It was a crude joke on the part of a couple of crude men.

▲ ▲ ▲

The Black Hole, across the inlet from Atlantic City, was the next program that I got involved in. It was short-lived, like most of the programs that I worked on, and not nearly the deal it started out to be.

After an uneventful run down to Atlantic City, I tied up at the state marina. The next day, way before daylight, I was on the road, and we were at the docks at the break of dawn. I got my boat loaded up and started, and ran across the inlet into the area known as the Black Hole.

What I found there was just that. Mostly it was one deep dredge hole without much on the bottom but grass and junk. The treaders were finding a few big clams, but most of us were not finding much.

I found a few smaller clams on the edge and started working my way along the dropoff, looking for a spot.

By noon I had only a few hundred clams, and stopped to eat my lunch. I watched as one bayman drifted in with motor trouble. He anchored up about fifty feet from me and worked on his motor. It finally started, and he went on his way without even trying the clams. After lunch, I went back to work and soon I was right where he had been broken down. To my surprise, I found my tongs full of clams. I anchored up so my boat could not move, and went to work.

It was a small spot, not much bigger than my boat. An old barge had sunk there many years ago, and the clams had caught there in good numbers.

I took in more than 5,000 that afternoon. Someone said I was high man for the day.

I stayed for about a week or so and went home. The travel gets to you, and if the catch becomes not too good, it's not worth the effort.

chapter seventeen

The Code of the Bay

A man's word was the most important asset that he owned.

It was an outsider who first asked me about "the code of the bay." At first I laughed, and then, after I had thought about it, I realized that there really was a code of the bay.

As time went by, I came to see that there was more than one code, and that the code you lived under was determined by the local culture. I can only surmise what the other areas had for a code of conduct. I will tell you a little of the code that I grew up under.

My father used to say that we were independent. By that, he was referring to a lifestyle, not a political party. It was a cultural norm to be dependent on the bay and woods for day-to-day existence. There was no other form of support that was acceptable to the bayman. There were no food stamps or welfare, although the county might lend a hand in times of need. The use of these services was frowned on by the culture, and the baymen avoided them except as a last resort.

The men I grew up around in my father's peer group were tough, honest men with a very strong work ethic. This was the way men were supposed to be, and to be lacking in any of these traits lowered one's value in the eyes of the Barnegat baymen.

The men were on the docks at the break of day, and a certain respect was shown to the man who was consistently the first on the water. Except when storms and gales blew, or the boat needed repairs, the baymen were on the bay. Most of them worked a half-day on Saturday unless they had lost time during the week. The truth was that the work required such a degree of physical fitness that to lose even two days in a row resulted in a drop in condition that could be felt the next day back at work. The loss of a week meant starting all over with aching muscles.

A man's word was the most important asset that he owned. Honesty among the men was highly valued. The liar might be tolerated around the dock, but he would have no friends among the core of the baymen who lived our unwritten code.

The thief, if such a one were to come around, was not tolerated. To be caught in the act would put the guilty party in fear of his physical safety. Once one was found out, he might as well find a new place to tie up.

When I was a boy and just learning to count and grade clams, Dad told me to put an extra clam in for each hundred that I counted. "The dealer will check your count," he said, "and if you are short, you will be given a new name. They will call you 'Shortcount' and you will have trouble selling your catch. If you throw the extra clam in, he will find your count over, and after a while, the dealer will trust you, and you will not have problems," he said. "Always sell the best package that you can, whether it is clams, crabs, oysters, or scallops. It is the best way for a bayman to go."

Years later I was selling to a dealer in Cedar Run, and he was counting some clams when I got in to the dock. "This damned Shortcount is 150 short today," he fumed. "He will be gone tomorrow. I will see to that." I felt kind of sorry for Shortcount. He had seemed like a nice fellow. But, he had been stealing money from the dealer, and I knew what was in store for him when he showed up.

The next night when I got in, Shortcount and his boat were gone. I never saw him again. Once this title is hung on a man, he has to go to some place where he is not known as Shortcount. No dealer would want to buy his catch when they found out his nickname.

▲ ▲ ▲

It is general policy that the bayman doesn't see, hear or know anything. He minds his own business. When government mishandles honest men, this is one of the outcomes. Fear of government that is well-founded produces a culture that will not interact with government, and a situation develops where the culture will exorcise a member for doing so.

Years ago, when the population was small and the waters were clean, it was common for the bayman to dump odd-count and small clams by the stern of their boat. In the fall when the weather got cold, they would have a day's pay or so in the water, right by their boat. As the years went by and the water's cleanliness around the docks was not guaranteed, this practice became illegal — the clams dumped there could be dangerous to eat unless well cooked.

I was the president of the Baymen's Association, and I was on my way out one fall morning. One of my favorite uncles was standing on the docks with his tongs, taking up clams that he had dumped by his boat.

I waved and went on my way. I wished he had waited until I was gone to finish his work. The practice had by then become illegal, and I did not want to be involved in any way. I felt that I represented the Baymen's Association and I did not want to bring dishonor on the group. I went on down to Long Point and from there I went about halfway down to East Sedge, where I was working. I had barely gotten my rake together when I saw the watchmen coming. There were about fifteen boats between us, and the watchmen ran through them to make a beeline for me. They seemed to be in a hurry, as they came at a high rate of speed.

I knew this was not a normal patrol, from this approach. They ran up to me and came alongside.

"Did you see anything illegal on your way to work?" This was the first question out of their mouths, and I knew I was in trouble. I had been critical of them at will, as I broke no laws and thought I was safe.

I had a dilemma, though, because I knew there happened to be clams in the water by my own boat. I had begun tying up at some docks that I rented from a private party. As opposed to using the docks of a dealer, this gave me the freedom to sell my catch wherever I wanted to. Also tied up at these docks were my uncles, friends and my brother, David. I had been working on my boat one day, and one of my small daughters who was with me wanted to go fishing. I took my tongs and made a grab by the stern of the boat. I was not disappointed to find there were quite a few big clams in the bottom, and I caught a few for her to use as bait.

So, on the day that I had seen my uncle, I realized the watchmen knew what I had seen, or they would not have asked the question. If I said no, I saw nothing, they would go back to Cedar Run and they would find clams by my boat, and by the boats of everyone else who was tied up at docks up and down the creek. Worst of all, they would discredit all the men in the association as outlaws. I was sure the watchmen were hiding in the area, and the newspapers would say I had collaborated in a scheme to sell unclean clams.

If I said yes, I would break the code of the bay and I would lose friends and family.

I think we had about a hundred members in the Baymen's Association and I could not bring disgrace and the title of outlaws on us all.

I said, "Yes, I did see something illegal on my way to work." I told them what I saw, and that there were also clams off the stern of my boat — clams which I had not put there.

I could see this was not the answer they wanted, and their little scheme to entrap me was not going the way they had hoped. They were nasty little men, and they showed it when they did not get what they wanted.

They started up their boat and roared back to Cedar Run without checking my boat or my papers. No one had ever been charged or penalized for this offense, and I thought the worst would be a reprimand for my uncle.

When I showed up at the docks to work the next morning, the watchmen were there in force. They had tongs and a Boston Whaler about half full of clams. I began to unload my truck and started toward my boat with my wire basket. One of the watchmen barred my way and said to me, "Did you see so-and-so tonging clams from these docks yesterday?"

All work had ceased, and the men who were there could hear what was said. The moment of truth had truly come for me.

"That's right," I answered.

"You know, we found quite a lot of clams by your boat," he said.

"I told you that," was my reply.

I had all I wanted of this person, and I walked around him and to my boat, thinking, let them do what they want. If they don't arrest me, I am going to work.

On my way back to the truck for the rest of my gear, I got to thinking about all those clams they had in their boat. "What will you do with those clams?" I asked.

"None of your business," they told me.

I figured they sold the clams and split up the money, else they would have been able to tell me what they do with confiscated clams.

A couple days later, my brother Dave called me with some bad news. "It's big trouble, Merce, they are going to fine us and take away our license to clam. Everybody but you, that is. All the baymen who tie up at those docks in that area had clams by their boat, and we are all losing our license," he said.

This was more than bad news; it was disaster. All those men out of work. I was so angry I could hardly see straight. They couldn't make an outlaw out of me to the state, so they made an outlaw of me to my culture.

The next day I got on the phone. The DEP (Department of Environmental Protection) was in existence and new heads were in the chain of command. I had made inroads at convincing some of them that all was not well on our bays.

I got to the man who could change things, and told him the truth: "These men are not outlaws. They are only doing what has always been done. They look at the clams; they look fine. They eat the clams and don't get sick, and they just did not realize how serious this is. They are from another time. Now that they know how intent the government is about this problem, you will not find them doing this again."

I pointed out that clams grow far up the creeks at times, and there was no way of knowing that nature herself did not put those clams there.

I told the truth when I was asked. "That man was my uncle. My only brother is among the men there, and some of the baymen I admire are there. If you do this thing as planned, you can take my name and stamp outlaw on it for the rest of my life," I told him, "and I will not talk to you ever again."

He told me to calm down, and not to worry. I thanked him and hung up the phone.

That was the end of it, almost. Nobody got fined, and there were no licenses pulled. The baymen there did not mention it, and seemed to understand the spot I was in. But my uncle never "saw" me again.

In my culture, when someone has broken the code badly, they are "not seen."

If the unseen one tries to talk to you, you ignore them. You walk away if you are approached. You never look at them; they are not a part of your world. You do not see them. When I saw that my uncle could not see me, I did the only thing that is left, and that was to not see him.

And so, I never saw one of my favorite uncles again after the fiasco at the docks. It was a high price, which I will continue to pay as long as I live. But, seeing a better system of government, with more understanding of the native, helped to ease my mind.

I believe not seeing a person who has broken a cultural taboo is found in primitive societies, in some religions, in fiction, and may be more widespread in modern society than we are conscious of.

I was not aware of the practice of not seeing in my culture until I started writing this chapter. I knew that I used it to handle outsiders who were violating my space or otherwise breaking cultural rules, but I did not see the role that it played in maintaining the code of the bay.

▲ ▲ ▲

"All the people need all the land to survive." I was reading a book that Listens-to-Whippoorwill, a Lenape chief, had lent me. I count the Lenape among my ancestors, and I think he wanted me to know more about my people.

It was like reading my father's words, slightly changed: All of the baymen need all of the bay to survive.

It was against the code of the bay to lease naturally productive bottoms. The practice of doing so removes the bottom from the use of the baymen in general. It was against the code of the bay to leave anyone, seen or unseen, broken down or otherwise in trouble on the bay.

It was very hard for anyone to infiltrate the culture. One reason was that we would not see them for a long time, or not at all, if the newcomer were to break too many cultural taboos.

The Barnegat Baymen were somewhat tribal, in that the town that you grew up in was your tribal area. There were Barnegaters, Waretowners and so forth, and this distinction was carried for life. I am a Forked River bayman.

Other areas had similar but different codes that they lived by. The code that you have lived by will always be the right one to the person who lives under it. It is not my intention to say what is right or wrong.

I am writing this only to give a glimpse into the past. Most of the men who inspired me to write this are no longer with us. Few, if any, of their descendants still work on the bay. With their passing, so goes the code of the bay.

It will be replaced by a new code. What that will be, I cannot say.

chapter eighteen

Politics and the Shellfish Council

I saw defeat on the faces of the Barnegat baymen and I carried it within me, hard and cold. I would do whatever I could to see the men responsible out of the system.

"**F**irst to fight for right and honor, and to keep our country free." It was impossible to march along singing this song for four years, and walk away from those principles when I saw them being violated. Once a Marine, always a Marine, they say, and I had a promise to keep.

There were two titles that were the emotional equivalent of "bogeyman" around the docks. They were "Shellfish Council" and "watchmen".

The council, as they were commonly called, were a group of men appointed by the governor of the state, who made the rules and regulations that baymen lived under.

The watchmen, or wardens as they were sometimes called, were the arm of the council that watched over the baymen and the business of the council. They were enforcement personnel.

When Dad and Edgar Barkalow were going out at night with their guns to protect the lots, I asked, "Why aren't the watchmen out there watching the lots?"

"The watchmen watch what they want to," was the answer. "A bayman on Barnegat has to do the watchmen's job also."

I decided I did not like the watchmen.

When I saw my Dad upset for days, along with the other baymen, over something the council had done or not done as the case might be, I further wondered what job these men were really doing.

That day on the oyster grounds when my father told me I did not see, hear or know anything about the massive-scale dredging allowed for a select few, I revolted. I swore that I would do something about conditions on the bay. I saw defeat on the faces of the Barnegat baymen and I carried it within me, hard and cold. I would do whatever I could to see the men responsible out of the system.

The first year I was married, 1964, was a busy time. I did keep a lookout for council meetings, but I always seemed to find out after the fact. That first September the word got out that the council would meet and set the date for scallop season.

I went, and the baymen were there in force. We sat there a while; the council members were late. It seemed they had dinner together before the meeting, and it happened often that the meeting would start late, I was told by the man next to me.

At last, they showed up. They were all grinning and they looked happy. The chairman opened the meeting and got right down to business.

"You boys are here about scallop season, so let's take care of it right away," he said. "The reports are good, and we will open the season the first Saturday in November. Any questions?"

There was little discussion.

At that point the chairman said we could all go home, as the rest of the meeting would not interest us.

To a man, the baymen got up and filed out of the room. I got up and walked out last. I was stunned that the meeting was over so fast, and shocked that all the baymen I knew had walked out.

"Why did we walk out like that?" I asked as soon as we were outside.

"We wouldn't be interested," I was told. "They transfer lots and do other things we are not interested in."

I was incensed. "Those new lots that used to be open ground don't interest you? I am not walking out of the next meeting," I told them, "and neither should you."

I began a campaign to incite the baymen against the Shellfish Council. This was not too hard to do; the council for years had been priming the pump, so to speak. All I had to do was point out this or that action they had taken. A large body of men was not happy with the way they were treated and the way the bay was being managed by the council.

It took a little while, but we finally found out when the next meeting was to be. I was very pleased to see the room filled with men as we waited for the council to show up after their dinner.

The council members showed up late again and wore a puzzled look when they walked into the room. The meeting was called to order and the chairman expressed surprise at the number of men in attendance. After all, there was no big issue to discuss. Why were we there?

Most of us felt there were many issues to talk about and we went to work on them. Everything, from the condition of the bays and stocks of shellfish, to the principles that were used to manage them, was brought up. It was a wild and hectic meeting.

When the time came to do the regular business, not one bayman left the room. We were all interested in everything.

I went home that night very pleased with myself. I had not gotten any promises for improvements, but I felt I had rocked the boat and broken the apathy.

I was learning a lot about the way things worked in the world of politics between the council and its subjects, the baymen.

The director of the council was a schoolteacher who had never worked the bays. Our representative for Ocean County owned a trucking company and was not a bayman. Some of the other members were old oystermen who had been on the council for years. When I asked how they got their seats, I was told they were there because they were successful oystermen who had made their money in the twenties. They were now old men of power.

I worked up a list of things that might be done in order to improve conditions for the bayman and the bays. Each time I learned about a meeting, I encouraged as many men as I could to go to the meeting and support the idea that the council had responsibilities to the industry and to the baymen. I felt if we could drum up enough support, we might be able to force the council to take a more active and middle-of-the-road posture in management.

It soon became obvious that this was a passive board that had its own agenda. Composed of men who did not physically work the water, and headed by men who were oyster-oriented, they were little interested in anything else.

When I asked why the council spent all its resources on oysters in South Jersey while Ocean County waters no longer had any oysters at all, I got a real surprise.

They said, "You have oysters. The state maintains preserves in Barnegat Bay where oysters are dumped and managed."

I nearly fell off my chair. I knew that there were, at one time, some areas called sanctuaries that oysters might have been dumped on. This was before my time and they were no longer marked, or staked, as we called it.

I told the council this, and they laughed. The chairman ignored my statement and went on with the meeting. This caused considerable uproar and it took a bit to restore order.

I persisted on the subject, and one of the members of the council answered me this way. He was red-faced and fuming. "Oysters!" he said, "You never saw oysters like your bay had. Why, in the twenties we hauled . . ." His voice faded out, as he realized what he had started to say.

Another member of the council, who was much given to long-winded descriptions of past oyster projects, picked up for him. This old man would talk at length aimlessly while the rest of the council sniggered behind their hands. "That's right," he said, "we took big dredges and dredged Barnegat Bay. We hauled barge-load after barge-load of oysters down to South Jersey."

The chairman, who was also an oysterman, interrupted him. Now was not the time for this discussion, he said, and changed the subject.

I felt like the cat about to catch the mouse. Some of the original rapists of the bay were sitting in front of me. I had not thought I would encounter the men responsible for the rape of my grandfather's time.

What these men did might have been legal, but it was morally and ethically wrong. It was a gross violation of the code of the bay. They didn't just dredge the shellfish out of the bay; they took the food out of the mouths of children. They made poor people poorer than they needed to be. They left a wound in the mind of the Barnegat baymen that had refused to heal.

As I sat there that night looking at them, I felt I was in the presence of the biggest criminals I had ever seen. The old man, who wanted to tell all, could be brought out again with a few leading questions, I was sure. The other old man was sharper and I would not get much out of him. I knew, without a doubt, that none of them should have anything to do with the management of Barnegat Bay. Now, for my grandfather's generation also, I wanted these men off the council. I resented the fact that the same men who robbed the baymen of their era still had their hands on the life of the baymen of my time.

In those days, the council met two times a year if I remember right, in the fall and in the spring. I had six months to think about what I would do.

In the meantime, someone told me about a big set of clams down by Barrel Island, and I went to take a look. The clams were there, but something else I found upset me and started a course of action that would change my life.

I found about twenty men down there with rakes that had been fitted with one-quarter-inch wire mesh. They were catching the seed clams and hauling them away.

It was always against the law to do this. The watchmen had a one-and-one-half-inch ring that they used to check the size of the clams on any boat they were inspecting. If a clam passed through, it was too small and illegal. If caught with undersized clams, a bayman could be fined.

I started asking questions about the rigged rakes among men on the bay.

"It has gone on for years," I was told. Some said, "You might as well go and catch the small clams, as they will die over the winter anyway." Others just said, "They do what they want to in South Jersey."

I went to the next meeting armed with a big old tape recorder. I set it up with a microphone, to try to record the answers from the council. I really was hoping to get the old man to say a few words about the oysters and the twenties. I was disappointed that he was not there. He had retired, they said with a grin. When I raised the question of the seed clams, I was told this was the way things were done. There was nothing I could do, they said.

Yes there was, I was now determined. The tape I made that night was useless, though. The meeting was noisy, leaving the tape too garbled to understand.

I wrote a petition, which I carried around the bay. In it the concerned baymen asked for a number of things, including the end of this practice of catching seed clams. At the same time, I tried to convince the men that we needed an organization to give us some unity if we were to try to change anything.

Nearly all the baymen I knew signed the petition and thought an association of baymen was a good idea. I set up a meeting at the Waretown Fire Hall and we agreed to form the "Baymen's Association for Environmental Protection." I selected this name because I felt if we protected the environment, we were protecting ourselves. I also felt that this would send a signal to the newly forming DEP — that we were working for the same ends and had the same basic goals. I was elected the first president and we set about getting our charter and becoming a nonprofit organization. We also began meeting with lawyers, assemblymen and various heads of departments who might be able to help us.

I wrote everything in longhand, and my dear wife Arlene edited and typed everything for me. She lent me her complete support, and along with caring for the family, spent many long hours at the typewriter.

Results did not come right away. This became apparent shortly into one meeting with an assemblyman representing Ocean County. I had hoped to get his support, and I had talked with him before about the seed clam problem.

"This is not happening," he said. "All my sources tell me this is not going on."

I pointed out that I represented a baymen's association and would not be there if what he said was true. He acted as if I was slightly deranged. It was obvious we would get no help from this man.

To his credit, he did not seem to be part of a conspiracy. It was more that he was a confused man who was not sure what to believe.

As time went by and I thought about it, I began to see a new picture of government. I began to see government as a sprawling entity. It is like a baby, only starting to grow. It sees, but not well; it hears, but only understands a few words. Its eyes and ears, in the case of our bays, were the council.

The state Department of Conservation and the Division of Shellfisheries dated to 1945, about the same time I was taking my first trips out on the bay with my father. A Shellfisheries Council was established within the Division. Prior to this, it seems that most of the laws concerned oysters and dated back to the late seventeenth and eighteenth centuries.

I had begun to see that unless we could convince government that its vision was faulty and its hearing was bad, we would not get much done. Government trusts its own. This makes the problem worse because the common citizens become suspect when they approach government with the suggestion that maybe it needs to improve upon itself.

Now I began to hear dire warnings of doom from those close to me. "Look out, they will get you," I was told.

When friends who owned a marina warned me that men were about, asking questions, I stopped laughing. I wasn't too worried, though. I was not an outlaw.

One of my cousins was worried about me for another reason.

"Why?" I asked.

"Most of the men who have ever gone up against the council wound up on their side. They all seem to get some nice lots and fade into the sunset," he said.

"Money is not the reason for my campaign," I told him. "I am for right and honor and to keep our country free."

"I hope so," was his answer.

There were some good signs on the horizon. The Wetlands Act was passed and the state now had the DEP. It was easy to see that the public was becoming aware of environmental concerns. We wanted to stop building on the meadows; so did a lot of other people. We wanted a clean bay. Who does not? We wanted an end to dirty politics and mismanagement of our bays. Who would not?

We managed to secure an appointment with the director of the DEP and the director of the Shellfish Council. There may have been a fourth member of the Baymen's Association present, but as I remember, Joe Reid, Stanley Cottrell and I went that day to Trenton.

The director of the Shellfish Council was the same man who had presided over the council in my youth. Here was the man who had caused so much trouble around the docks. In the long run, here was the man who was responsible for my father and his mates taking their guns out on the bay after dark. This man presided over the "oyster fiasco" in the late fifties, and I had promised myself that I would do whatever I could to see him off the council.

The meeting started on a friendly level and quickly degenerated as the council director tried to pass off pat answers to the new head of the DEP. In all fairness, the council head did fairly well until I asked him about oysters in Barnegat Bay.

After council members told me that oysters were being dumped and managed on the sanctuaries in Barnegat, I searched out maps and located them. I went to the areas in my boat and searched them. No oysters, not one.

I did not go to the council and tell them this. It was a piece of evidence I would hold until the right time.

When the director of the Shellfish Council began to tell of the oyster project in Barnegat Bay, I was silent. When he was finished, I asked how the oysters did on these sanctuaries.

"Fine," he replied.

I let him have it with both barrels, as they say on the bay.

"There are no oysters on those sanctuaries, and there have not been any there for years," I said.

I was not alone; Joe and Stanley both knew this to be the truth and backed me up. The director of the council lost his composure at this point and the meeting soon ended.

I was on pins and needles as I waited for the next meeting of the council. I was not disappointed; we had a new director. The old director was now the assistant director, who sat there and did nothing. I was not too happy that he still held a title, until someone said, "How humiliating to have been the director all those years, and now be the assistant." He came and sat at a couple of meetings, and I never saw him again.

I had taken some care that my motives were hidden. The old director of the council never knew why I warred against him for about five years or more that it took to see him off the council. My goal had never been vengeance, only to see him gone.

There were some more postive changes on the council. I began to see more members, such as a state biologist, attending the meetings and being represented on the board. The more eyes and ears looking out for an organism that cannot see or hear, the better off it is.

I should have been able to rest at this point. My long-ago promise to myself had been kept. However, I had opened up a can of worms. I seemed to be offended in some way at each meeting of the council I attended. I became aware that the Barnegat bayman lived under a different set of rules than some of those who stood to profit more.

It is understood that the state owns the waters of our bays. It is the law that these waters can be leased to private parties for growing or storing oysters and clams.

When Mom and Dad had the clam stand on the highway in Lanoka Harbor, they sometimes had clams that did not sell. Not having a lot, as leased ground was called, we had to dump these clams back in the bay in some secret place. If someone found them, they would be gone.

Dad applied for a lot off Forked River and was given a small one. I questioned him one day about the allotment procedure, when we were in the garvey on the lot. Dad was using a pair of sixteen-foot tongs to take up some clams we had dumped that summer. There were some other small lots there, all about the same size and belonging mostly to Edgar Barkalow, Bernie Penn, Frankie Penn, and a couple of other men whose names I cannot recall.

The lots were well offshore, the wind was up, and it was mean there. "The lot had to be in this area," Dad said. "There are a few clams in closer to shore, but a lot must be where there are no clams. The watchmen come and look for clams, and if they find any, you don't get the lot."

It was a tough rule, but I could see the sense in it. It would keep natural areas and good growing areas from being leased by private parties and thereby becoming closed to the baymen.

Early on, I tried to use these rules to block the transfer of some lots. They were surrounded by natural and good growing areas that contained large numbers of clams. This implied that the lots themselves were natural clam grounds and should not be leased at all.

The chairman of the Shellfish Council called me a fool.

"Why would anyone lease ground that didn't grow clams?" he asked. "We sent the watchmen out to check that the area is good for raising clams. If it checks out, we give him the lot."

Please, bear in mind that the chairman that night was the last old oysterman from my grandfather's time. He was sitting there on the council when my father and his mates got their lots.

"You mean to say that after you made my father and his mates put their lots where there was nothing, the waters are rough, and they cannot be watched from shore, that these are not the rules?" I questioned.

"It is the opposite; you only lease out good growing ground. That has always been our policy," he said with a smile.

A picture came to me of my father, as he balanced himself on his one good leg and worked the sixteen-foot tongs that cold winter's day on the lots.

I would hound this man all I could, until he was gone or I was. If I saw him smile at all, I found a reason to attack him. In fact, I kept a whole bag of fresh approaches just in case he should smile; this was another of my little secrets.

It was four or five years later at a council meeting that he threw up his hands and said to me, "What do you want? You can have anything you want."

I told him, "I want a clean bay with fair and just management for all. I am for right and honor and to keep America free."

He got a disgusted look on his face and threw up his hands again in a gesture of defeat. I never saw him again that I did not try to harrass him some more with words. Since I was not having any luck getting rid of him, I tried to exact justice whenever the opportunity arose.

By 1976 I was serving on four executive boards: The Baymen's Association for Environmental Protection, The Commercial Fishermen's Council, The Coalition for Survival, and The Pinelands Cultural Society.

One particular month, I had a long stretch of meetings in a row. For ten nights I was off to a meeting of some sort, and that had been the general trend for some time. One night I was sitting on the bed and pulling on my boots for another meeting, when one of my daughters came in.

"Could you please give us a ride tomorrow night?" she asked. It was some school function that was very important to her. As I sat there looking into those intent blue eyes, I got the impression that I really had not seen her in a long time. She looked at least six inches taller than she did the last time I had seen her. I made her smile right away when I told her she had her ride.

It was as if a fog had lifted and I could see clearly for the first time in a long while. The most important people in my life were my family and that was the most important area of my environment.

As gracefully and as quickly as I could, I resigned from all of the boards that I worked on. I took some time to assess my situation and decided that the music would get most of my attention.

I did not attend a meeting of the Shellfish Council for a number of years. Then, I was approached by someone who wanted to know if I would consider hauling boatloads of chowders out on the bay to be dumped on lots as part of a plan to increase the fertility of the bay.

I attended my last meeting of the Shellfish Council to ask some questions, as I was considering doing the hauling job.

My first question was, "Why chowder clams? They are at the end of their life cycle and will be dead in a few years."

Much to my surprise, I was told that chowder clams do the best at producing spawn. I replied, "That makes the hard clam the only organism I have ever heard of that does its most successful reproducing in its geriatric stage of life. Some fish, such as salmon do, but it is a once-in-a-lifetime occurrence. With the hard clam, reproduction is a seasonal activity."

They nervously agreed, but assured me it was so. I sensed another can of worms, and dropped the subject. I surveyed my boat and found she was not in shape for the project, and so I had nothing more to do with the Shellfish Council.

At the last meeting I attended, in 1986, I found the board to be expanded. Ocean County still did not have a representative who was a well-rounded bayman. I believe that the baymen should be represented by someone who is, and has been, an experienced bayman. As of 1999, that has not been the case.

I was able to walk away from the politics of the bay because I felt I had done my part. The old director was gone and it was right. I had fought for the honor of my grandfathers, and for my father, and that was right.

I have had no contact with this board for more than ten years now, and I hear nothing bad or good about them. Their meetings are open to the public and should be advertised in the local papers. I urge those who are interested in the well-being of our bays to attend.

chapter nineteen

Treasures from the Bay

I have lived the life of a free man, and that is the greatest treasure that a person may acquire.

A "Turlington" bottle found in the bay.

Over the years that I worked on the bay, I was able to acquire some treasures. It was a childhood dream of mine that I would catch a gold bar one day. That was never to happen, but I did find gold, both real and in analogy.

From the time I started with my father until I retired from the bay, a total of thirty-seven years passed. During this time I scraped and dug at the bottom of the bay and I caught some unusual and sometimes thought-provoking objects.

The oldest were, of course, the stone tools that sometimes surfaced after tens of generations. I returned the majority of them to the water. I did keep a few, which I still have. They are among the treasures that I love the most, as I feel they are from my ancestors.

When I was a boy and Dad got the fiddle out, he would "rosin up the bow." When he did this, it was with rosin that came from the bay. He had several chunks of the amber-colored substance he had caught while working in the water. They really were chunks of hardened pine pitch or sap.

Rosin was used, he said, in the caulking of old sailing ships. He thought an old ship had sunk in the bay at one time, and the rosin had been lost with the ship.

I was working in the deep water off Tices Shoal one day when I felt my rake hit something hard. It rolled into the rake. When I saw what it was, I was amazed. It was a cylinder-shaped piece of rosin, about eighteen inches long and about eight inches in diameter.

What was unusual was that the shape of the original container could be seen. The rosin had been poured as liquid pine pitch into a seal skin. The shape of the head, the eyes and neck — it was a perfect cast until it had broken off cleanly, the rest of the original package remaining on the bottom.

There were no museums at that time that I knew of, so I stored it away in a cool place. After a year or so, it sagged out of shape and I gave it to my brother Dave, who agreed it was the biggest single piece of rosin he had ever seen.

I do not recall ever catching rosin anywhere but in Barnegat Bay. For that reason, I do not think that the native Americans were the peoples who left the rosin in the bay. It would have been more widespread.

However, it is from a much earlier and far more primitive time than ours that seal skins were used as a form of container. I still carry a piece of rosin from the bay as a good luck charm when I play music out.

▲ ▲ ▲

By far the most common evidence of bygone years that I found on or in the bay were old bottles.

Some spots we worked were full of old bottles, some older than others. I dated them this way: If the bottle had the ring on the neck, cast along with the bottle, it was not too old. If the bottle had been cast in a mold or blown, and the ring applied after, it was older. Other indicators of age are defects in the glass and the shape of the bottle.

Some of these old bottles had round bottoms, and Joe Reid told me they had held a soda-like drink.

All of the bottles become worn from the action of the saltwater on the glass. An iridescent film forms on the inside of the bottle. This, I have read, is the result of water dissolving the glass.

Some of the shell piles in upper Barnegat have not been worked in seventy or eighty years. They are still holding the artifacts, such as old bottles, which the baymen of long ago left there. It might be that some areas in the upper bay are archeological sites.

The bottle I like the most, and one of the oldest, is a small, green, fiddle-shaped bottle. It reads: "BY THE KINGS ROYALL PATENT GRANTED TO ROBT TURLINGTON FOR HIS INVENTED BALSAM OF LIFE."

I gave many bottles away to friends and family; I still have a couple of dozen that I like to look at.

▲ ▲ ▲

Most things are not too durable in saltwater. It tends to eat up iron . Brass, lead, copper, silver and gold all do a much better job of withstanding the action of the saltwater.

Over the years I caught pocket knives, pocket watches, butter knives, forks and spoons. Certain areas where the people fish or sail, they lose things overboard. Fishing poles of all kinds come aboard. Most of this stuff is in pretty bad shape; the saltwater has been eating away at the iron.

By the time I went off to the Marines, I had lost count of the number of anchors I had snagged. Most of them were of no use to me, as they were too small for a bayman's needs.

Between High Island and Egg Island in Little Egg Harbor Bay is an old channel that we called the Dog Hole. When I was working there one wintry day, I lifted my rake and noticed the gleam of gold. At first I thought it was a piece of costume jewelry. On closer examination, it appeared to be a gold chain with a small spoon about three inches long dangling from it. On the way home I stopped at a place that bought and sold gold to see what I had. The man looked it over and told me it was a gold cocaine spoon and chain and he would give me $185 for it. I had thought to keep it, but when he told me what it was worth, I decided to take the money. It was a lean time and we loaded our larder with the proceeds.

▲　▲　▲

I caught a revolver off Forked River Point. It was very rusted and I would have liked to keep it. I took it to the police in Forked River and never saw it again.

Among the stranger catches was a .50-caliber machine gun shell that I brought up from the bottom of the Dog Hole. It lives in my shop and is slowly rotting away. I was afraid for a while that it might explode, and I did not want it around my family.

Working down off Long Point, I caught what I thought was that elusive gold bar. At least I thought that for a short time. When I lifted my rake I spied an ingot of some type of metal. Its weight was about three pounds and I could see the gleam of gold where the rake had scratched it. Otherwise, it was black and had been roughly poured.

When I checked it out, it was brass, much to my disappointment. I keep it around and refer to it as my "gold bar" to this day.

▲　▲　▲

There were other treasures that the bay gave to me, but I did not always see them as that at the time. Hindsight makes things much clearer, and sometimes the greatest gold is experience with people.

As the years went by and larger boats sailed the reaches of Barnegat Bay, I found myself more and more of a curiosity. Folks out for a sail were interested in what this fellow in his garvey was doing.

Some sailed by at a decent distance, cast a good look and went on their way. Other skippers seemed to feel if they passed more than ten feet away, they would miss something. I would be standing there working, and along would come a thirty-footer, in a fair breeze, with all her sails up. As the boat got closer, I could see it was going to be one of those close inspections. I would begin to wonder, does he see me? Or, will this be the time my poor old garvey gets sliced in half?

As time went by, I was getting more and more angry with people who had no respect for my personal space. I began to use meditation as a means of coping with a situation that I had no control over.

The first step was to realize that they had no effect whatever on my life. The only way I could tell they were real was from the wake they left, and that was small.

I began to not see them. If they wanted my attention, they would have to run over me. When I got one of those close inspections, I did not even turn my head. I would hear the sound of the boat passing and feel the wake — I knew they were real, but they were not interesting to me.

One hot summer's day, a sailboat passed close to me and I looked; I don't know why. I hadn't checked one of these boats out in a long time. What I saw startled me, to say the least.

It was a pretty boat, about thirty feet, but it was the crew that was the most interesting. In the stern, at the helm, was a lovely and quite naked woman.

Amidships, and also naked and lovely, was another woman. Last but not least, on the bow deck, with no more on than her sisters, their counterpart knelt.

Together with the boat, they made an altogether compelling picture. I took a good look, and, unwilling to be manipulated by sex or sailboats, and determined to be a gentleman, I turned back to my work as if nothing had happened.

My sometimes-photographic memory had been activated, however, and I still can see them sailing along. I considered them to be a sign from the Great Spirit that I was on the right course. Anyone who would not regard this experience as a treasure would be wrong.

As I grow older, the greatest treasures are the "do you remember when we did this?" times. Friends and family will prod my memory and I will find myself carried back to the days when we went out on the bay for some of the best times of our lives.

With hindsight, I know that to have lived a life of a bayman, with my days and hours dictated by the elements as ancient man must have lived, was a treasure indeed. I have lived the life of a free man, and that is the greatest treasure that a person may acquire.

Philosophy of the Bayman

*Each of us has our hands on the
helm to steer the ship.*

When I was working out on the bay, if you had asked me
about this or that, I would have told you what I knew or believed about
the subject. You would have gotten an oral history along with a liberal
dose of my philosophy.

I have written this book in the same spirit, as if I was talking to you
one day out on the bay.

What do I hope to do by writing this all down? Some of my goals should be easy to see. There is no doubt about right and honor and keeping our country free. But also I want the reader to see the bay waters from the perspective of the value it would have as unpolluted resources. In this chapter, I also present a few suggestions.

All of us are aware of some degree of pollution in the bays. Strides toward environmental purity have been taken, but there is more to be done. Cleaning up the visible pollution in our waters alone will not do it. Next must go the contamination we cannot see with our eyes.

▲ ▲ ▲

I read an article some years ago about the bottom paint that is used on fiberglass hulls. It said the paint contained a certain compound that, at levels of two or three parts per million would kill mussels. The study did not include other shellfish, but I would assume it was a hazard to them also. I hope by now it is no longer in use, but in any case, bottom paints are destructive of marine life. They have to be, to be any good. They are called anti-fouling paints and are designed to deter growth of marine life.

If the paint would stay on the bottom of the boat, everything might be fine. I have read that water is the universal solvent. It breaks down the paint, and the poisons are leached out into the surrounding water. Along with that, the high speeds that many boats are operated at tends to tear the paint off the boat through friction.

I am told that a great deal more care is given in the marinas these days toward keeping bottom paints out of the environment. That is all well and good, but think about this: If you were to total the bottom area of all the boats that are in the water on any summer's day, in all the marinas, creeks, lagoons, and the bay itself, you would have acres of bottom paint. If there were a man-made island of that size anchored out on the bay, with its bottom coated with a highly poisonous substance that was leaching out into the water, there would be a great public outcry. Because we only see one or a few boats at a time, we do not think about it.

What is the philosophy here? Is there a true need for all this poisonous paint to be in contact with the surface of the bay at all? I think the answer is no. For the majority of the boating public, the use of toxic bottom paints is not justified.

What happens when you do not put copper paint on your boat? Copper paint was the term we used on the bay to describe bottom paint. I would pull my boat out in the spring and the bottom would look like a glass bottle. Every sign of bottom paint would be gone, worn off by the winter's ice. One spring I was catching a good amount of clams and kept putting off my spring haul-out. As the summer got closer my boat got slower and my gas consumption got higher. Under the boat I could feel barnacles about the size of marbles. I discovered that as long as I ran slowly, my fuel usage was slightly over normal. Any attempt at speed burned a lot of gas real fast.

As soon as the water was warm enough, I got overboard on the flats with our garden hoe and scraped the bottom as clean as I could get it. Forty-five minutes later I planed out and ran on in to the dock. I did this again at the end of the summer, and the first ice I ran through in the fall took care of any barnacles I might have missed.

That year I did not use any toxic bottom paint at all. In bygone years when the boats were of wood, bottom paints were also used to protect against shipworms. They eat holes in a wood boat. In all fairness to the shipworm, however, they were not common prior to the Oyster Creek nuclear plant, and they do not eat fiberglass.

I would guess that the largest single class of boats today is fiberglass, less than twenty-six feet, spending only a few months of the year in the water. Do all these boats really need to be treated with a toxic substance? Or could the owners store the boat out of the water, or scrape the hull a couple of times during the season? This would inconvenience boat owners somewhat, but it would remove a source of contamination from one class of boats.

What about larger boats? Most of them don't go anywhere anyway. What difference does it really make if your bottom has barnacles if you never take the boat out?

Mike at Cedar Creek Marina in Lanoka Harbor said to me one day, "You know, you are the best gas customer we have."

"What do you mean?" I asked.

"You buy more gas than any boat here," he said.

I looked around at all the big pleasure boats and pointed to a forty-footer. "I burn more gas than he does?"

"Most of them just sit on the boat and only go out a couple times a season. You go every day all year."

The Cedar Creek Marina does not grow many barnacles, because the water is too fresh and does not have enough salt in it. None of those boats really needed to have toxic paint on their bottom.

Years ago, in Forked River, John Lewis had a boat yard and mixed his own bottom paint. Red pepper was part of his recipe. It should be possible for others to make organic bottom paints that work without introducing chemicals into the environment that are lethal to fish and shellfish. John's bay garveys were prized as strong and good-looking boats.

If any boats need high-tech bottom paints, it is the commercial boats and the Marine Police or Coast Guard boats.

Some folks might say, why should I clean the bottom of my boat twice a year? Instead, I will just get rid of the boat. Others will say there are too many boats on the bay, anyway.

To that, I ask, do we save a little work and poison the water, or do we bite the bullet and clean up our bays?

In some cases, such as the Oyster Creek Nuclear Generating Station, more than cleaning up is involved.

As I mentioned in the chapter on oysters, the plant had such a thirst for cooling water that it has drawn the water in the Forked River upstream. The flow has drawn in a considerable amount of bay water, also. Along with the bay water, any spawn from fish and shellfish can be drawn into the plant's system. Once in the system, most of the spawn may be killed by entrainment, entrapment, or impingement in the plant's cooling and filtering systems.

I lived about three blocks from the Oyster Creek, and I used to walk down to my boat at about daylight to go to work. I noticed early on that large clumps of some foamy-looking matter would be floating downstream. I mentioned it to some of the marina owners on the creek and they said it came from the chemicals the plant used to clean marine growth off the plant's systems.

It made sense — they would need to clean marine growth off the underwater pumps and other gear. They have a lot of saltwater coming through. I have read that if the bay were closed off, the plant would completely circulate the bay's contents in three and one-half days.

I was at a meeting of the Commercial Fishermen's Council and someone had gotten hold of a study of all sources of pollution, the type and amount that was being discharged along the northern New Jersey coast. When my turn came to study it, I was excited. Now I would know what those large, floating clumps of matter were that I had been seeing in the mornings.

I was surprised and disappointed to find only "(secret)" where that information should have been. I thought that was scary, and I still do.

The Ciba-Geigy plant in Toms River had a long list of chemicals that it was allowed to release into the bay and an even bigger list of chemicals that it was sending into the ocean. How many of those chemicals are toxic to marine life? Is this why the bay is dead off of Toms River?

What is the philosophy here? Do we let large commercial entities destroy our environment while we do nothing? The "farm" to which I earlier compared the bay belongs to us all, and if we don't take care of it, we won't have it. The risk grows that we will poison ourselves as the buildup of toxic waste continues.

I do believe it is wrong to introduce toxic waste into the environment. I believe it is wrong to degrade the environment in any way that we can possibly avoid.

When we build on the meadows and fill in the wetlands, we degrade the environment and damage the overall fertility of the bay. We pay lip service to environmental concerns, but the building does not stop. It disturbs me to see new houses on the bayfront. I would like to suggest it is time to think about tearing them down.

Why would it be such a radical idea to think about filling in some of those lagoons, getting rid of the houses and restoring the wetland areas to their natural state? We may need to if we are ever to restore the bay to its natural state. Why would that idea raise more concern than forever killing a variety of species of marine life?

Not only does the fertility of the bay suffer from all those houses covering the meadows, but the runoff of chemicals and phosphates into the bay is also highly detrimental to the marine life living there.

We all want cleaner waters. What I would like to know is why we do not adhere to our own wishes. Why do we allow local and other branches of government to sell us out and allow building on our wetlands?

▲ ▲ ▲

For the baymen of my time, it is a double tragedy. Not only do we have an unproductive bay, but also we have also lost the use of the wetlands that were a part of the bayman's life. At times or according to the season, they were a source of income, food and even fuel for the stove.

My people were religious and did not work on the Sabbath. That meant there was one day a week that was open to recreation, after church on Sunday morning.

My brother and I used to head for the woods. It was about a mile through the woods to the meadows. The route to get there passed through swamps where the flies and bugs would eat us alive in the summer. When you got out on the meadows, though, the afternoon breeze would clear the air. Most often it would be the prevailing southeast wind off the bay. As you got closer to the water of the bay, the temperature of the air dropped. We spent many happy summer afternoons roaming the bayfront.

And so the meadows were a source of recreation to the bayman from the time of his youth. As I grew older and began to work on the bay, there was less and less time to enjoy idle days. It became more important to get the day's work done than to satisfy an urge to take a walk or to catch soft crabs.

Never mind, I would say to myself. I will not work forever, and when the time comes, I will do as I did in my younger years. I will feed myself from the bounty of the bay and the meadows. That, I said, will be my reward for years of hard work. I will build myself a nice duck boat, carve a set of stool ducks and set them out when the northeast wind blows. I will feast on the broadbill and black duck.

All this and much more I promised myself. As the years passed I began to see it was never going to happen.

What we did not lose to the developers we lost to government programs that bought up large tracts of wetlands in order to preserve them, and then banned us from going on them. If I want to shoot or walk, I must get a map and see where I am allowed to go. Much of the land is off-limits. Along with the loss of land went part of the baymen's cultural legacy.

I believe that in order to be a philosopher, one must be able to detach from the thing one is thinking about. We cannot allow our thinking to be influenced by emotions, or we will not be able to think clearly, and we could reach the wrong conclusions.

For that reason, it took me a long time to be able to write about the bay. I started to write this manuscript many years ago, but I could not finish it. It was too emotional and I was too attached to the past. I am many years and 450 miles gone from the bay now. Since moving to West Virginia, time and distance have given me the detachment I needed to think about my life and the water that I loved so much.

When next you look at the water, I want you to be a philosopher and consider what is and what is not to be for our bays and wetlands. When you look at the houses marching across the wetlands, consider the view without them as it was in the recent past. Remember what has been. We can reclaim it as it was. Is it possible that future generations could see not only the cleaning, but also the rejuvenation of our bays and wetlands?

What about a long-range plan, perhaps a 100- or 150-year plan? At the end of this time, all houses and sources of pollution would be gone. No more gasoline-powered boats, just sails and electric. What a wonderful gift to the future that would be. Few if any of us would see the completion of the plan, but we would have the satisfaction of seeing the journey started.

What about the remains of the culture that is left? I am talking of those baymen who filed their income taxes and can prove they worked on the water as their primary means of support. They and their descendants deserve to be considered in any long-term plan that is developed.

There will always be a culture on the bays; what it will be like will be determined by events that shape the future. Already there are great changes from the past. It is becoming a culture of fiberglass boats and young men who have little knowledge of the bay and its history. As the old baymen pass out of the pattern of things, the old culture with its love of the water is lost.

What the future will bring is hard to see. It is possible that the bay of the times to come will be entirely mechanized. Giant dredges and corporations may replace the bayman and his work boat. I hope not. I prefer to believe the bayman will survive. That ideal will need the support of the public and the government to make it so.

One of the first steps might be to declare New Jersey bays to be endangered ecosystems in a state of emergency. A moratorium on commercial licenses is needed to protect both the bay and the baymen's future. Licenses could be issued based on a criterion of a proven history of bay work. Once a base number of commercial licenses is reached and current baymen have theirs, no more would be issued until shellfish stocks warranted a larger number.

Stabilizing the number of commercial licenses would help the bay by ending the gold rush syndrome. Otherwise, each time there is a major set of any stocks, it is overwhelmed by public pressure. Everybody is after the quick buck.

If, for instance, the Cedar Run flats were found to have a good growth of clams next summer, there would be two or three hundred boats working on them. By the end of summer, the stocks would be gone and along with them the fertility of the bay. The stocks do not get much chance to reproduce, and that has been one of our biggest problems. We need only to improve environmental quality and Mother Earth will bring it to life over time.

▲   ▲   ▲

One winter I noticed Dad had a decoy in the gear he carried painted like a seagull. I did not ask right away the reason why, as I liked to figure things out on my own if I could. Finally I gave up. I just could not come up with a reason to do such a thing. I asked about it.

He laughed and answered, "We are having some troubles with a watchman who calls some friends up north whenever we get a spot of crabs. If he sees a buoy out, he takes our ranges and the next day, there they are. So we painted up some seagulls and use them for buoys. Our buoys are just seagulls resting on the water, and it is much harder to get the ranges on us."

It was a good idea that worked, but it should not have been necessary. When I started out on the bay, they were the watchmen, and as time passed, they became the Marine Police. More time passed and they became part of the State Police. I was overjoyed. The state troopers were well spoken of by the baymen in general. To me it meant the caliber of the men who enforced the law on the bay would rise. I hoped that a stricter code of conduct to which they adhere would mean an end to some of the bad practices that had gone on in the past.

No one who enforces law on the water should have any financial interest in the commercial activities that they monitor. There is too much potential for abuse or for charges of abuse. No enforcement officer should pull up alongside a bayman and inspect his catch as a means of determining where he or his friends should go to work the next day. They should not lease lots and neither should they buy or sell the stocks that come from the bay. Besides the moral reasons, I feel certain that enforcement officers are paid more than the average bayman and should not be competing with them. The state Marine Police should be above reproach in all matters. I have reason to say I am not satisfied that this is the case even at this writing. It may be that this is an area of government that still needs a little work.

Government will ever be evolving. It is the public that determines the direction and speed of change in a society. If you want the future to take a course toward environmental purity, action by the public is the only thing that will make it happen. I do not now, nor have I ever condoned illegal or violent activity. What is to be done must be done in the spirit of peaceful and legal progress.

Each of us has our hands on the helm to steer the ship. Non-involvement is simply letting go of the wheel. If our ship is wrecked, we are all to blame.

chapter twenty-one

Genealogy

Compiled by Arlene Martin Ridgway

The Stuyvesant place in Bamber. Merce, Sr., with guitar; Bill Britton, Elsie Britton, Sarah Britton (in doorway), and Myrtle Ridgway.

Merce's ancestry is English on both sides, Lenape on both sides, and Dutch on his dad's side. The English part is very well documented; the Dutch part less so, and the Lenape is oral history.

Since 1976 I have been collecting bits and pieces of family history as I became aware of them, and through the kindness of others who were also collecting. There are many worthy publications in the area to look in for data. I give credit to these works and folk who so kindly helped me out.

In 1993 a different publication concerning the Ridgway genealogy came to our attention. Merce was working with Dan K. and Joanne Myers

*Above, left to right;
Merce's maternal
grandparents, Thomas
Taylor, Jr., and Pheniah
Penn Taylor; paternal
grandmother Wilhelmina
Leek Ridgway. Left, Great
grandfather Capt. Joel
Haywood Ridgway and
the crew at the Barnegat
Life Saving Station.
Below, left, Grandpa
"June"; Merce's parents.*

of Asante Productions of Minneapolis to produce a video, "Pine Barrens' Son."

Joanne found a 1926 edition manuscript in the Minnesota Historical Society's archives titled *Descent of the Ridgway-Ridgeway Family in England and America*, by George C. Ridgway of Evansville, Indiana.

His earliest information was gathered from one of Britain's most famous and oldest documents, the Domesday Book. It was compiled between 1085 and 1086 to survey every manor in England and tax the landowners. The following is adapted from George C. Ridgway's compilation.

Ridgway Descent

Leofric I., born about 680, was the first earl of Leicester, earl of Lincoln and earl of Chester. He was a member of the royal family of the Kingdom of Mercia.

Leofwine, fifth earl of Leicester, married Alwara, granddaughter of Athelstan, first king of all England. His eldest son, Wulfric, married Elswitha, sister of Elfric, archbishop of Canterbury, was slain by the Danes in 1010.

Leofric III, earl of Leicester, earl of Northampton and duke of Mercia, married Godiva, countess of Coventry. Even today, the name "Lady Godiva" still survives. Her historic ride was to protest her own husband's high taxes, and out of respect, her people didn't look.

Leofric was captain-general of Canute's army, grand master of the Freemasons, and superintended the construction of Westminster Abbey. He founded the monastery of Coventry.

Eadwyne, eighth earl of Leicester, was fourth and last duke of Mercia. He had three sons; the eldest, Asser, was progenitor of the Ridgway family and son-in-law to William the Conqueror. When Eadwyne was slain by a large force of Normans, William declared that "the death of this brave and benevolent noble was the greatest calamity that England had sustained."

Genealogist George C. Ridgway noted that he was greatly indebted to a man fifteen generations removed from Leofric I, Sir Thomas de Rydeware, for the account of the family, which Thomas prepared in the year 1308.

The story of the family lineage continues with varying spellings. In different periods and localities were found eight different forms: Ridwar, Rydeware, Rydgeway, Wrydgway, Rudgwy, Ridgwaie, Ridgeway and Ridgway. Early genealogists attribute the different spellings to peculiarities of the early English pronunciation.

It is noted that Sir Thomas Ridgeway, first earl of Londonderry, of Torrwood Grange and Torre Abbey, was knighted by Queen Elizabeth as Golden Knight. Historical accounts label the distinction "a new and peculiar honor, seldom being granted by her."

He was the only member of the family using the *e*. His father and his sons used the shorter, Ridgway.

As a sequence of the early colonizing in Ireland by Sir Thomas Ridgeway and many of his family, we have large numbers of Ridgeways (with an *e*), while diligent search fails to reveal an Irish Ridgway without an *e*. In England, the contrary prevails.

The Thirtieth Generation

When the lineage reaches the thirtieth generation from Leofric I, the backdrop is set for a venture to America. Robert Ridgway, fourth son and youngest child of the second earl, was the father of Richard the Emigrant, baptized August 24, 1631 at Torre Church. He married about 1653. He had one son, Richard, born 1654. Richard the Emigrant was to succeed as fifth earl of Londonderry, but renounced his right because of his Quaker principles. He married Elizabeth Chamberlayne (or Chamberlain). They emigrated to North America on the ship *Jacob and Mary* in 1677.

They and their firstborn son Thomas arrived at Burlington, New Jersey. At that time, Burlington County extended the width of the state. They settled on a farm across the Delaware River in what is now Pennsylvania. He was engaged in farming and cattle raising, and gave one acre of his land to the Society of Friends for a meeting house. In 1700 he is listed as one of the judges for Burlington County, an office he still held as late as April, 1720. He died in 1723.

Richard and Elizabeth had seven children: Thomas, Richard, Elizabeth, William, Sarah, Josiah and Joseph. She died in 1692.

Richard and his second wife, Abagail Stockton, were married February 1, 1693. She was the daughter of Richard Stockton, who with his wife and eldest children had emigrated from England prior to 1660. They first settled at Flushing, Long Island and later moved to Burlington County. He was the grandfather of Richard Stockton, signer of the Declaration of Independence. Richard and Abagail also had seven children: Job, Mary, Jane, Abagail, John, Joseph, and Sarah. Four children, from both unions, died in infancy — William, both Sarahs and the first Joseph.

The second son of Richard and Elizabeth, who also bore the name Richard, was married twice. It was one of his sons who settled in Barnegat and established the line from which Merce descended. Richard was married first to Mary Willits, daughter of Hope and Mercy Willits of Long Island. His second wife was Mary Crispin, nee Stockton, who was a younger sister of the elder Richard Ridgway's second wife. (The father and son married sisters.) The younger Richard died in 1718, leaving six children: William, Timothy, Elizabeth, Richard, Mary, and James.

In the year 1729, Timothy Ridgway married Sarah Cranmer and made their home in Barnegat, according to *History of Little Egg Harbor Township*, by Leah Blackman. *Out of the Past — A Pictorial History of Barnegat, New Jersey*, reports that "the first to purchase land from the proprietors was Levi Cranmer and Timothy Ridgway." For twenty shillings in 1759 they bought 500 acres along what is now East Bay Avenue. From this tract of land was deeded in 1770 the "one acre and half quarter" of land on which the Quaker Meeting House had been built in 1767. Timothy Ridgway built his dwelling across from the meeting house grounds.

From the book *Ridgways, U.S.A.*, written by Gertrude Brick and compiled by Lillian Arnold Lopez (Lillian had a Ridgeway ancestor), we learn that Timothy and Sarah Cranmer Ridgway had a son Richard who married Lavina Bird. Their son, Peter, and his wife, Edith, bore a son Joseph B., who married Phebe Pharo. Joel Haywood Ridgway, their son, married Mary Catherine Inman of the Inman whaling family who pioneered Long Beach Island.

Joel Haywood Ridgway, Merce's great-grandfather, held the post of keeper at the Barnegat Lifeboat Station on the north end of Long Beach Island. Captain Ridgway was appointed in February, 1876 and served until 1899. The book *Under Barnegat's Beam* by Bayard Randolph Kraft recounts that the men never knew when circumstances might call them into the frigid foam to rescue survivors of massive, wrecked ships.

The second son of Joel Haywood Ridgway and Mary Catherine Inman Ridgway was Joel Haywood Ridgway, Jr. He married Wilhelmina Leek and they had three children — Joel, Viola and Merce's dad, Maurice Inman Ridgway, who married Myrtle Taylor.

Myrtle remembers that Wilhelmina's mother, Sara Jane Lemmon, was a full-blooded Lenape, and that Wilhelmina was half Lenape and half Dutch. Dad recalled his mom telling about her going into the woods to gather her medicines.

Myrtle's dad told her the story of a father and some young men out riding in the woods looking for deer. They found a Lenape girl; she was alone and hiding. They captured her and took her home to safety. The family accepted her as one of their own. Eventually she married one of the young men in the family.

Myrtle's father, Thomas Taylor Jr., was known as "June", and her mother was Pheniah Penn. Merce's great-great-grandmother was Almira Walling, who was a full-blooded Lenape and an orphan.

Merce's father, Merce Ridgway, Sr., was born in Barnegat in 1915. Barnegat was then a small village nestled between the shores of Barnegat Bay and the thick woodlands of the Pine Barrens. Around 1920 the family relocated to live in the village of Bamber.

Although Merce, Sr. was primarily a bayman, he had also mossed, burned charcoal, and worked as a machinist. He was a carpenter who built his own boats and a noted folk musician. His songwriting spanned forty years and his songs were heard on the airwaves and in performances at such locations as the National Folk Festival in Washington, D.C.

This brings us to Merce, Jr.

The Pine Barrens Song

I left the place where I was born
   Many years ago
For times were hard, work was scarce
   I had no choice but go
But I've been back there many times
   In my memory
Of all the places that I've been
   It's there I'd rather be

Chorus:
Where the scrub pine, ground oak,
   Berry bush and sand
They never change, they never will
   Pine Barren land
The sweet maypink, curly fern, and
   Leaves all turning green
And the water running red,
   In the cedar swamp stream

Pine smoke from the wood fire
   Blowing on the wind
Lamplight in the window,
   Shining once again
One room schools, country stores,
   The folks we used to know
But times have changed and they were gone
   A long, long time ago

Repeat chorus.

Wagon roads that run for miles,
   Down through the twisted pines
Past little long forgotten towns
   That failed the test of time
And sometimes there along the way
   Granite markers cold and grey
Mark the only ones to stay
   There in the barrens,
Pine Barrens

— Merce Ridgway, Sr.

The Bayman's Wife

The difficult parts are easy to remember; they stick like glue, the glue of living and surviving. The job of a bayman requires long hours and total dedication, a true commitment.

By Arlene Martin Ridgway

Having an Irish great-grandfather who clammed in the Raritan Bay, a father who sailed the world, a first husband who fished the ocean — seemed normal to me that twelve years later, as a widow, I met Merce and we married.

A positive aspect to being married to a bayman was that he worked for himself. Because baymen are individuals, they approach their occupation in individual ways. They could make their own schedules and their own hours, so one bayman's workday could be unlike another's.

Merce did not have a nine-to-five job. He was completely at the mercy of the elements, which directly decided when and where he would work. So did they decide suppertime. Supper would not be at the standard 5:00 p.m., but anywhere from three to five o'clock. A strong wind could end the workday early, but in summer, it might be seven o'clock before the bayman sat down to dinner. It gets dark late that time of year, and legal clamming hours are from sunrise to sunset. So a wife learned, as a cook, to be ready for all possibilities.

The negative side to working for yourself is that if you have morals and integrity you may, and often do, work too many hours instead of fewer. You need to "do it all." So, family members also become involved in the enterprise, and this changes the family's dynamics. Everyone learns how to work together, which means taking each and everyone's ideas as viable. As a family, every one of us, regardless of age, had our parts to play in keeping the family ship afloat and shipshape. There were eight of us, and that many different schedules, and we all had our responsibilities.

All in all, it was a very busy, interesting, educational, adventuresome life, and never, ever boring.

The difficult parts are easy to remember; they stick like glue, the glue of living and surviving. The job of a bayman requires total dedication, a true commitment. It is what you call hard labor, achieved by pure determination and a strong body. It takes many skills: at certain times and under certain circumstances, one wrong move and you're fish bait. Never knowing exactly when your mate will return in the evening from a day of work can be trying.

Things like the weather that might not mean much to some workers, may to the baymen be the beginning and end of it all. Baymen are always looking for a good weather station on the radio or the television; or listening for weather reports from anyone talking about it. To this day he keeps an eye on the weather.

I never knew whether Merce would come home tan and smiling, or windblown, or fog blind, or cold to the core. I remember one time when he had been working in the fog for about four days. Every evening, we each related the highlights of our day, but with the bay business and six children, you get in what words you can, and some of that doesn't always sink in. He went off to work on the morning of the fifth day, smiling; it was a beautiful sunny day, not much wind. I turned to the next agenda of the day and about a half-hour later, I heard a car pull into the driveway. I looked, and was surprised, for here came my honey, back home again.

Knowing him and his diligence, I was curious why he was home. Did something break down?

He said with a smile, "Come on, get in the car and take a ride with me down to look at the bay."

I was a little baffled, and answered, "I have housework to do."

"You can still do it, just take a few minutes and take a ride with me."

Wanting to humor him, I went along. Well, you could have knocked me over with a feather when we got to the bayshore. There was no water, there was no sky, and there were no boats out on the nonexistent bay. No sea gulls, nothing; nothing but one huge curtain of thick, dense, white fog.

I had never seen anything like it. On one side, the sun was shining brightly; the sky was blue with lovely white clouds. On the other side, like a giant hand had reached up and pulled it down, right at the water's edge was a thick, puffy, white curtain of fog.

I looked at Merce and laughed and said, "I sure see how come you are home. You've been working in this for four days? How in the world did you manage to do that, anyhow?"

I had some idea of what he had been enduring, for he had taken me on a boat ride to Brigantine one foggy day. What a trip that was. We could only see a few feet ahead. It was as if the garvey was encircled. Out in the whiteness we could hear engines and the lapping of the water. Merce had to rely on his good hearing, his compass, and his experience. We rode all the way to Brigantine and back, and never saw anything except for a few feet of water around us.

It was eerie, engines sounding like they were bringing their boat right to you and on you and through you, but never coming into sight; and voices drifting in the mist.

I was sure glad to head up the home crick and to the dock. My eyes felt deprived and eager to be able to see into the distance.

If Merce had not been the experienced expert that he was, I would not have gone. It takes an expert to be able to work in such conditions, and I trusted him and his boat. I also now understood "working in the fog."

Each season had its particular challenges, so the bayman lived by the seasons in this respect. In the summer, he tended to leave early to take advantage of the morning cool.

Nasty weather was a continual challenge. The lightning was one of the most scary conditions, to me. Merce would tell me, "When the hair stands up straight on my forearms, I disconnect my rake and get in the cabin."

I've watched him from the car walking sideways down the dock in a gale to check the tie lines and the pump. The wind was blowing so hard it looked like it could pick him up and throw him anywhere it darn well felt like. I remember when he had only a hand pump, and it took what seemed like hours to keep the garvey pumped out. A lot of times it happened in the evening after a day's work, and in the pouring rain. Then he bought an electric pump and that helped a lot, but he still had to keep an eye on it to make sure it was working. If he was lucky, he had at least been able to get some supper in his belly.

Winter was the most worrisome, work-filled season on the water from my perspective. The ice, the layers of clothes and rain gear, keeping the boat from sinking, keeping the boat from banging against the docks when the winds blow — simply staying alive — was a constant challenge.

I kept Merce company on one of these winter expeditions. He was docked in Cedar Run and the ice threatened to damage the boat, so he had to stay there and monitor the situation, no matter how long it took.

It was night, dark and cold. The bigger children were at home keeping an eye on the younger ones, but we took the baby with us. It was nice and toasty in the car — the baby slept peacefully and Merce popped in and out, checking the ice levels for hours. Finally, all was well and we went home and to bed. Morning came early that next day.

The boat was a seven-day-a-week job, regardless if the weather was fit for shellfishing or not. The garvey was an extension of my husband. It needed constant monitoring, pumping out, having its tie lines adjusted and batteries brought up, and on and on. It was used constantly, so it needed constant care. So even if he got Sundays off, he still had to go check the boat.

In fact, when the weather got bad, they were on the move, the watermen. In the old days, folks understood this; in modern times, not always so.

No one could argue with working out in the open when the weather was fine, though, and it was on many, many days. I would look at Merce and say, "I need a break, can I go out with you to work tomorrow?" That was when the older children were big enough to care for the young ones and when school was out.

He would work as usual, and I would read, write, stare, meditate, and help sort the shells. I steered on the way home so he could count his clams. A ride out in the bay with Merce was a renewal of spirit for me.

The family fun that we had with the garvey was another positive of being married to a bayman. The garvey fulfilled our business obligations and it also provided some of our recreation. On nice days we went fishing, crabbing, treading, swimming, picnicking and collecting.

I remember one terribly hot July day. It was absolutely stifling, not a wisp of a breeze, and humid — "hot and hummin" is what the natives used to say. Merce decided, "Let's take a ride out in the bay; maybe there is a breeze out there that will cool us off."

It was a wonderful ride as long as the boat was moving, but as soon as we stopped, the heat and humidity grabbed us again. It was, amazingly, no cooler than it was on land. So, we followed our next idea, to find a sandy piece of beach. We pulled the boat in as far as she would go and anchored securely. Then we all got in the water, and we crawled around, staying three-fourths submerged and looking for shells and little critters and special stones and pieces of wood for the rest of the hot afternoon.

We snacked on a cooler full of goodies I had packed and went home in the cool of the evening. It had turned out to be an afternoon of science for us — a negative turned into a mighty-nice positive, and a pleasant family time together.

The bay was an educational tool, a research lab. We used the woods in the same way, loading the car up with everybody, riding out in the pines, and letting the kids spread out and feel the air and the pine needles underneath their feet. We could listen to the quiet of the woods and find its treasures — plants, critters, old bottles.

One early spring weekend day, we took everyone over to Long Beach Island and to Barnegat Lighthouse. When we got to the beach, all the children took off at once, running across the sand, all spreading out like a big fan. We couldn't help but laugh. They really needed that, after a long winter.

Then there were expeditions that didn't turn out so well. The kids named one of them "Bug Island." We needed a break, so off we went for a boat ride. The plan was to go down by Brigantine and camp for the night. We even had our hound dog with us. Well, we arrived, after a long ride, to find the wind blowing in the wrong direction and the air full of flying insects. We tried to stay and have a little fun, but it was impossible, so we turned around and rode all the way back to Oyster Creek, just getting out of the boat and into the car in time for a downpour.

After that, being home was much more appreciated than when we had left!

Then, there was another time that Merce drove us over to LBI, down the Beach Haven end. We took a nice long walk down the beach, all the way to the end of the island. He kept looking up at the sky and making comments, "See those clouds? We may have to turn around and go back."

The sky was sunny. I couldn't read in the sky what he was reading. We reached our destination, and he said, "It's coming faster than I thought. We have to turn around and go straight back."

We had planned on staying and looking around for treasures, hermit crabs and shells, but that was not going to happen this time. So, off we took up the beach in a row. The big girls helped carry the little ones. It got cloudier and darker as we hurried. We just made the car and all climbed in when it started to hail — large white hailstones, maybe an inch in diameter. We sat there, slightly wet and laughing and mighty glad to be sheltered, while the hail beat down on the roof of the car.

These are the things I remember the most. The fun times, the good times, the exciting small adventures.

Our life was a balancing act, centered around my husband's bay schedule, the children's school times, and the schedule of "the musician," a different plan yet. It seemed as if anything could happen at any time, and it usually did. Our oldest, Tom, says:

"I remember one deer season, the telephone rang about eight o'clock in the morning the second day of the season. My mom answered it, and it was the truant officer wanting to know why I wasn't in school.

All she said to him was, '#$%@ *&#$!!, it's deer season!' and hung up. It was the greatest thing my mom could have said. The truant officer never called again during deer season."

Somehow, we managed to keep things rolling along. I wrote lots of notes and signs, and many, many lists, and fit my schedule around theirs. When things didn't go the way we planned, we'd improvise and hope for the best.

I was born in Perth Amboy, and moved to Forked River in 1949. I lived in South Jersey for thirty-eight years. Through those years I met a great many interesting people, quite a few unusual characters, and a few liars and thieves — your normal mix, no matter where you go. I was accepted by most and "not seen" by others, who still considered me to be "an outsider." I got used to it, and learned to live with it. The people were neat, different. I think it was because of the rich, varied history, and the many traditional occupations that were practiced there. They were dramatic, creative, diverse, interesting people, and incredible storytellers!

They wrote poems, too. I found this in an old notebook I kept. Our family communicated by notes quite often; this was one Merce left:

Honey and Jen,

Good Mornin'
Mocking birds calling, calling to me.
Whippoorwill singing his dawn melody.
Up in the morning, first break of day,
I'm going clamming, out on the bay.

Love, Merce

Recipes from a Bayman's Kitchen

Crockpot Deer

3 pieces deer meat (part of the ham), about 4 pounds
1 cup water
$^1/_2$ teaspoon salt
4 medium onions, chopped
4 medium potatoes, peeled and quartered

Remove tissue layer from meat. Put meat, water and salt in a crockpot with onions and potatoes on top. Cook on high for 6 to 6 $^1/_2$ hours. *Serves 6-8.*

— **Robert Thomas Gille, Jr.**

Merce and his brother Dave with a snapping turtle.

Snapper Soup

Cut hole in near toes, tie to wash line, cut head off. Bleed overnight. Scald with boiling water to remove skin. Cut around shell where it meets skin. Remove guts in one piece. Remove lungs. Cut meat into six pieces: neck, four legs, and tail. Boil until meat can be picked off bone, approximately 1 hour. Remove meat. Cook all vegetables in broth; carrots, potatoes, onions. Flavor with cloves, salt and pepper. When vegetables are done, put meat back in and serve.

— **Lemuel Eastburn**

Note: One good-sized snapper will make a large pot of soup. Use 2 carrots, 2 potatoes and 1 onion. Serves 6-8.

Clam Stew

Cook minced clams 3 to 5 minutes. In another pan, boil milk. Add milk to clams in a soup plate. Add butter and pepper.

— **Gilbert Wallace Gray**

Note: That's clam stew for one. Half a cup of clams and their liquid plus 1 1/2 cups milk will do it.

Cranberry Wine

8 quarts cranberries
8 quarts water
5 pounds sugar

Wash and chop, or grind, cranberries. Dissolve sugar in half of the water, warmed. Bring to a boil and pour over cranberries. Add the rest of the water, cooled. Let sit for about 2 weeks to ferment. Every day during that time, stir the berries through a jelly bag. Squeeze dry and return to kettle or crock for another week. When this week comes to an end, siphon liquid into clean bottles. Put corks in lightly, for it may keep working. Be certain fermentation is finished before corking tightly. Try this with Thanksgiving dinner. *Yield: about 10 quarts.*

— **Bob Dittman**

Pickled Green Tomatoes

When I was a kid in Forked River, I recall the crock of pickled green tomatoes that stood behind the door where we could help ourselves to a tasty treat on cold winter evenings.

My mother put them down each year when the suspicion of frost drove us to pick off all of the tomatoes that would be lost to freezing weather. Her method was simple. Wash and dry the tomatoes, taking special care for perfection and the stem end being free of sand. Pack in a deep crock with several sprigs of dill weed.

Boil a gallon of water and in about a pint of this dissolve a cupful of kosher salt. Return to boiled water with a few cloves of garlic, peeled and split, and a few peppercorns and bay leaves. This she cooled before she poured it over the tomatoes in the crock and covered it with a plate weighted down with a rock.

As I recall, we weren't allowed to touch it for several weeks.

— **Lillian M. Lopez**

chapter twenty-three

The Music

*Added to all of this were the strains of
music drifting out of the hunting cabin.
We were in the right place after all.*

*The Pinehawkers at Albert Hall. Back row, from left: Joe Horner, Dave Gant and son,
Mike Ahearn, Glenn Borden, Lenore Franzen, Tom Gille. Front: Arlene and Merce.*

When I was a boy we had a wind-up phonograph. One
day, for reasons that I do not remember, my parents put it on the enclosed front porch of our house. I pestered Mom and Dad until they
said I could play it.

It seemed to me that it was only a few minutes until they said I could
not use it. I could not understand why. It was a long time until they let

Top, left to right; Sam Hunt, Bill Vath and George Albert at the Homeplace.
Above; Merce, Jr. and Sam Hunt.

me play it again.

When I asked my mom about it years later, she said, "Well, Merce, to tell you the truth, you scared us! For three days all you wanted to do was play that phonograph. You wanted to do nothing but play the music."

I was startled, to say the least, for in my mind what been a short time was really three days. I have always been possessed by music. That was driven home by what she said, and I understood a little better how much the music had hold of me.

The first time I hear certain tunes, and sometimes for the first several exposures to the tune, I am moved to tears. Some music generates feelings of sadness, while other music brings on joy or nostalgia.

When I was recovering from rheumatic fever as a young boy, I played on the fiddle, mandolin, ukulele and guitar. I don't think I learned to play much, but I passed a lot of time with music. To this day, I lose track of time and find that hours have passed as nothing while I am playing music.

Grandpop June was said to have played just about all instruments, though I remember him mostly for the mandolin. He was credited with a good memory for notes.

There was a piece called "The Great Cove Time," which was played around. Grandpop remembered from hearing it played on a passing barge, and brought it home where it was picked up by local musicians.

My father was a songwriter of some repute, best known for "The Pine Barrens Song." Dad had enjoyed listening to his mother sing the old songs. He bought his first guitar, a Bradley Kincaid, from Sears and Roebuck. A teaching booklet came with it. He and a friend kept at it, learning to play. He began playing and singing with two of his friends with whom he had burned charcoal, Bill and Walt Britton. Walt was his brother-in-law and Bill was Walt's cousin.

About 1941 they were approached by a folklorist by the name of Dorothea Dix Lawrence. The researcher had come to the area looking for local folk musicians. She inquired at the post office in Forked River and was directed to the "Bamber Boys."

She met them and asked if they would be interested in performing publicly with her acting as their sponsor. They agreed.

The group, dubbed "the Pinehawkers," received good press. They performed on radio stations WQXR, WNYC and WOR, for the Composers and Conductors Association in New York, for the Stephen Foster Lecture Theme Program at the Berkeley-Carteret Hotel, and other locations. They were introduced in 1941 at the National Folk Festival in Washington, D.C.

In 1990 I made a tape with Marimac Recordings which contained much of my father's music.

▲　▲　▲

I went on playing music the whole time that I was in the Marines. I met a fellow from Alabama, Gary Hager, who finger-picked the guitar and played old tunes that I loved, like "Maggie," "The Sheik of Araby," and "Wildwood Flower." He was without a doubt one of the best guitarists I have ever known, and played a large role in the style that I use today. After my discharge, I was looking around for musicians to play music with and I spotted Phil Grant playing music on the beach at the middle lake in Forked River. After that, we got together whenever we got the chance.

One night he said that his father had talked to George and Joe Albert, that they had music at their hunting cabin in the Waretown pines and we were welcome if we wanted to come.

We made our way on the next Saturday night out through the woods to the hunting cabin. It has been well over thirty years since that night and as I remember, there were present Joe Albert on tub bass, George Albert on fiddle, Sam Hunt on banjo, John Peich on harmonica, Bill Vath on guitar, plus Phil and myself with our guitars.

Along with these folks, about a dozen others who were there to hear the music made up "the rest of the gang," as Joe Albert called them. About 10 o'clock, we stopped the music for cake and coffee in the kitchen. Many of the ladies had brought goodies, which I learned was a standard practice. We soon got back to playing music and did not stop until about 2 in the morning.

From this point on, I knew where I wanted to be on Saturday nights.

Arlene soon had to see what I was doing and became a regular also, along with Phil's wife, Karla. I was to meet many other musicians over the years that I went out to the Homeplace, as we began to call the hunting cabin in the woods. Some were locals, and more and more it was also folks from outside the area.

The group that was playing that night, along with Jim Camburn and Jim Stackhouse, were known as the Pineconers. Joe Albert named the group and they had been playing out for years under that name.

About two years into this routine, Phil and Karla went off to join the Peace Corps. Arlene and I continued to go to the Homeplace. I also played the following summer at a coffeehouse with Dave Rinear from Bonnet Island.

Because I had grown up listening to my father's music on the radio, it was the most natural thing in the world for me to close my eyes and compare ours to what I heard on the radio. I knew it was not all good, but some of it was great, and I knew without a doubt that it could be set before the public and received well. In the beginning when I tried to convince others of this, I did not find many who were of the same opinion.

When Dave and I were playing at the coffeehouse, we would show up early for our set. Many times as I sat there listening to the music, I was sure the forty-five-minute sets were too long for some players who were not that good. I thought that twenty minutes would have been about right. Needless to say, there was much discussion with Dave about the presentation of music and the possibility of organizing the music in the pines at some point in the future.

I knew that better music was being played out at the Homeplace, although I knew the same problem existed there in a way. The music had no form and some of the musicians could not help but try to monopolize the music. As Pete Curry said in his Homeplace song, "twenty tunes without stopping for air."

Looking back now, the Homeplace holds fond memories from those years.

Finding it that first night was something of an adventure. Out Route 539, across from the area where Wells Mills Park is now, was a dirt road that ran back into the woods. Along the way were road signs that people had brought in from other areas, and here and there, people had leaned mirrors from dressers up against trees. At length we came to an intersection marked by a construction that we came to call "the phone booth." Inside was a stuffed animal of some description, and other oddities, which in general created a feeling that we were in the wrong place.

It was starting to get dark as we drove into the parking area, and the deer were walking all over the place. Joe and George had a number of foxhounds, and they began to howl and bark. Added to all of this were the strains of music drifting out of the hunting cabin. We were in the right place after all.

We got out our instruments and went inside.

The kitchen was clean and neat with a wood cooking stove, gas lights glowing and a gas refrigerator. There was no electric. A hand pump on an old-time sink and a table with some chairs completed the picture.

Beyond was where the music was going on. The main room had bunks around the outside walls, and inner layers of chairs filled with friends and musicians. The walls were hung with pictures and memorabilia of hunts. There were some sayings that they had hung up, my favorite being: "Bad breath is better than no breath at all."

And so for about fourteen years we went to the Homeplace. I was to watch it grow and grow, and meet many musicians there on Saturday nights. Some of these, such as Lewis London, from South Jersey, were great and I had thought to be seeing them on national television by now. Some were not so great, but sheer ego seemed to carry them on.

People brought their youngsters, who would fall asleep on the bunks as the music played — shades of my childhood.

The old folks would sing and at least once a night we would play some polkas and make a little room for some of the gals who liked to dance. Most notably Janelle and Naomi Stackhouse, along with my wife Arlene, were the polka dancers.

Phil and Karla came back from Afghanistan after a couple of years and we all continued to go to the Homeplace on Saturday nights. I was surprised how many of the people that I met were connected with the bay and made all or part of their living there.

During these years I watched as the numbers of people who came on Saturday nights grew. Musicians from all over and folks from all over would come out for the music. Bill Vath stopped playing and managing The Pineconers and new people took over that job. George Albert, the fiddler, passed on and Joe continued the music at the cabin.

▲   ▲   ▲

I forget the year, but some time during the later years of the Homeplace, my distant cousin, Russell Horner, organized some of the musicians in a show at Southern Regional High School. He was the first I saw to organize the music into a comprehensive form.

It was starting to get pretty weird on Saturdays at the cabin. I found it unnerving to look at the windows and see them filled with the faces of those who came for the music, but could not get inside for lack of space.

The last time I went on Saturday night, I had to park a long ways off and walk in with my guitar. I found at least three groups were playing on the grounds for a big gang of people who were milling about and drinking beer. There was another group playing on the porch, another group playing in the kitchen, while the main room and music were filled to capacity.

I sadly walked back to my car and went on home. There were far too many people as far as I was concerned.

I stopped in to see Joe that week. "Merce," he said, "I am going to have to stop the music. It is getting to be too much for me. I get up on Sunday morning and pick up five garbage cans full of beer bottles and cans. They are stealing my fox hides and other things. They are fighting in the woods and I am finding needles. It has to stop."

I was not surprised. Sad, yes, but not surprised.

As a group we all felt a great loss and none of us knew quite what to do. I found myself hanging out at the Dry Dock Inn and talking to other musicians who had no place to play, either.

Phil Grant and I began to discuss organizing a regular show at the community hall in Forked River. No positive steps were taken, and six months passed without any real movement.

Arlene and I used to go on Friday nights to the Waretown Auction. Here we would buy our rolls and eggs for the week and walk about looking at the wares that the various vendors had for sale.

Earlier that summer, the wife of owner Scotty Howard had stopped me and asked if I played music with a certain group. I replied that it was true; I sometimes played out with this particular group. "We are interested in having music here in hopes of bringing more people out on weekends," she said. Would I ask about them playing there and find out how much it would cost? I agreed and talked to the group leader.

When I told Mrs. Howard that the group wanted $500 a night to play, she said that was too much and I had to agree. We were both disappointed, but there was not much we could do about it.

So that Friday night we were looking for eggs and rolls and not much else. As we were walking about we happened to meet Mrs. Howard and stopped for a short chat. It was a rainy night and I was surprised to find they were not having the auction and business was very slow. "You need to have some music," I commented to her as we were having our little chat. She surprised me by taking me by the arm and saying, "Talk to my husband."

She led me into the auction room where Mr. Howard was working on some gear. "Mr. Ridgway wants to talk to you about some music," she said, and Mr. Howard and I began to discuss the possibility of putting together some type of a show.

I told him that I knew quite a few folks who used to go to the Homeplace, but now had no place to go. He said that the Friday night auction was not going well, and that night was open. The floor of the room was littered with the leavings of the crowd from the previous Saturday's auction. The room was unfinished with a small platform that the auctioneer used. "We do not open during the week and you will need to come in early to clean up and you will need to clean up after your show," he said. "The rent will be seventy-five dollars a night; can you handle that?" I thought we could but I needed some time to think about it.

Arlene came in the room and we walked around thinking. We talked and I felt the work involved was too much. "I don't think we should do this," I told her. "We will be working our butts off and this is not the best place to play music."

She looked at me and said, "If you don't do it now, it will never get done and the music will die."

I saw the project much as I saw the overboard man. Whatever was to be done needed to be done now, and I loved the music too much to let it die. I told Mr. Howard we would need to discuss it with my family and after that I would call him.

We talked to our children and they said they would help. I called Mr. Howard back and told him we would go for it, and a date was set for November 29, 1974. We also agreed to continue the show if it was successful.

Arlene and I talked and it was decided we would work as equal partners in this venture. We each had our areas of responsibilities, but her word was as good as mine.

I started calling musicians and this was the basic plan we offered: On November 29, we were putting together a music show at the Waretown Auction. We were getting in touch with as many of the musicians from the Homeplace as we could, and any who were interested were welcome to sign up for a twenty-minute set. If the show was successful, we would try to do it the following Friday night.

The goal we were after was the building of a music hall and the establishment of a nonprofit organization to administer the music.

Arlene and I had read Artur Rubinstein's *My Young Years* just prior to the passing of George Albert. In it he describes touring the music halls of towns and cities in Europe. We had been talking about a music hall for the music played at the Homeplace. We all knew it could not last forever, and it was getting too big for the cabin in the pines.

At George's viewing, we mentioned the music hall idea to Pete Curry and he suggested Albert Hall as a good name — "They have one in England, you know."

George Albert passed away on October 31, 1973; it wasn't until 1974 that the first real steps were made in the direction of Albert Hall.

It was a basic tenet of the agreement with all of the musicians and support staff that some effort would be made to pay the musicians or reward them in some way for their performance. I also made it clear that we needed some form of compensation for our phone calls and other outlay. It was, however, the first priority to pay the rent and other immediate bills from the small gate proceeds. All agreed that we would have a zero tolerance for alcohol and other drugs. We all felt alcohol had played a strong role in the ending of the music at the Homeplace.

I drove to Joe Albert's to have a talk with him. He was sitting on the porch and invited me in. After some small talk I told him what I was up to, and what we were going to try to do.

"Merce," he said, "it's all yours; all I want to do is come play and have fun. I don't want anything to do with the rest of it."

I told him that would be just fine and we changed the subject. Because of this, Joe Albert is not listed as a planner in the original brief report that we wrote about the origins of the Albert Hall project.

I knew that most of the musicians were as tribal as the baymen. Some of them were baymen or the children of baymen. Much has been written about the isolated culture that was found in the pines and shore area, but in truth, we were a general culture with many subcultures within.

As I began to call and talk to the musicians, I encountered as many different attitudes as there were musicians. Some said they did not think it could be done; others were enthusiastic. There were those who said they were afraid that a certain group would take over and it would become their show. One group leader said, "See my manager," and would not talk about the plans at all. I was later to hear them say in public that they were the founders and had started the project.

There were forty-eight people involved in that first show. Thirty-three were musicians who played that first night; thirty-four were people that I listed as dialogists. By that I meant that they participated in conversations about the show, incorporation, the music hall and/or other facets of the project.

Now it began to get really hectic. We had about three weeks till show time and much to be done. The phone was busy till late at night with conversations about the project. The support staff who would be doing the grunt work — the gate, security, and clean-up crews — were mostly our family and friends, and would fall under Arlene's direction. Stage, sound, program, and so forth would be my primary responsibility, and in an emergency, either would fill in for the other.

We needed a flyer so that the public would know about the music and hopefully come to listen. I engaged my friend, Phil Grant, to draw one, and I asked for a fiddler on the cover. When I went to pick it up, I found myself looking at a beautiful picture of me playing the guitar. Time was short and the flyer still needed to be printed and gotten out. I hoped the people would not think it too pretentious, and headed for the printer's.

As zero hour approached, the activity became more and more frantic. The phone was busy day and night. Arlene fielded for me while I was on the bay and I went to work when I got home at night.

The musicians were funny folks, and they had last-minute worries like we did. Some were only too glad to play, and all wanted to help build a music hall in Waretown. Some were worried about the lighting; some were worried about the sound. Some had yet other worries about their performance. Arlene and I did our best to shore up those who needed it. It was, after all, a big step. Playing on stage is a far cry from playing music in a hunting cabin in the woods.

One morning we woke up and it was the day of the show. We went over to the auction building about midday and started getting ready. It wasn't long before the staff showed up and we all got busy with details. The chairs were moved, the floor was swept and everything put back in place and dusted. Tables were made into gates.

One group had made it plain that they would not play looking into bright lights. Others had voiced concern over lights that they were not used to. I got around it by installing a clear lens in one of the kids' Lite Brite game and hanging it from the T-section of my shinnecock handle over the stage.

The young men who were the security section were to look for prob-

lems and all the people involved agreed to function as one large polic-
ing agent. In the event of a major problem, I had lots of backup.

The people began to arrive and it was finally time for the show to
start. The room had begun to fill and soon we were out of standing
room. It was packed with folks who had come to hear and be a part of
the music.

From that point on, the memory is dreamlike. The music . . . the
crowd . . . time passes too fast . . . the performers must be gotten on
stage, on time . . . sound levels must be checked.

As hard as it was to believe, we had no major problems and the music
played, even though we were quite busy chasing out the drinkers.

Oh, how the music played and the crowd roared their appreciation.
It was unbelievable. They shook the rafters and made my hair stand up.
Others told me they had the same experience. The music was, indeed,
well received.

The auction room was only a part of a much larger building which
was broken up into small shops that different folks sold their wares from.
I had made arrangements with Mr. Howard to allow the musicians to
use some of the shops that were empty as tune-up rooms. The overflow
crowd from the show was out wandering around listening to the various
groups as they jammed and got ready to play.

I set up a system where performers would sign up for the next show
and we had no problems setting up the program for the following Friday night. I designed a program that would allow folks to sign up weeks
in advance, and many did.

I saw and heard music and performances that night that I have never
again seen the equal of. Perhaps it was the roar of the crowd that inspired them.

All at once, it was over. The show was finished and we were all in a
state of shock and still hyperactive. We had asked all who could to stay a
short while and help us clean up. The response was incredible. A gang
of workers started grabbing chairs and moving them so another gang of
sweepers could do their job. Such a cloud of dust and banging of metal
chairs! Others were returning tables and other sundry items to their

resting places. The tune-up rooms were swept and in about an hour the place was shipshape.

As we headed home that night, the moon hung big and full over the road and we decided to make the short drive down to the bay and look at it. It was the perfect capper. I looked and took it for a good sign, moonlight dancing on the water, the end of the show.

When I tried to sleep, however, the show would not come to an end. My head was filled with music and I had barely gotten to play. The night was so filled with chores and responsibilities that there was little time for my own music. Sleep would not come and I got up and played my guitar until the day was spreading its light on the land.

This was to become the pattern of our lives for some time to come. Along with making a living from the bay, the music was to become all-consuming to me.

Now that the first show was over, we had to do it all again in one week. I had helped us out by getting the musicians to sign up in advance. I still worked until late at night on the phone, and I was getting a variety of reactions. One group leader told me flat out he didn't think I could do it again in so short a time. Most, however, were quite supportive and assured me they would show up on time to play.

Many of the musicians were not too happy with the Friday night slot for the music and I felt the same way. The music in the woods had been on Saturday nights and, in truth, it is better that way. Most folks are done with the week's work and a night off is in order. I told them if the music was worthy, it would soon occupy the Saturday night slot; that we were off to a good start; have faith and play hard.

In the blink of an eye, it was Friday again. We started around noon to clean up the room from Saturday's auction. The staff drifted in and soon we were all hard at work. The afternoon disappeared into the show, which started early. The room filled up and we were "standing room only." The crowd still roared, but not quite as loud. There were still people in the rest of the main building, but not quite as many.

My biggest problem that night was the drinkers. They floated in with their jugs and cans and we told them to take it out. Most left peaceably, but some balked. About the third time that the security had to come get me, I got a real surprise. Someone from the local law enforcement was sitting there with an open beer and did not want to leave. I knew his father, and him some, and they seemed like regular guys. "I'm sorry, but you have to take the beer out," I told him.

"Aw, Merce, you know me; it's okay."

He was in the back and it was dark back there. The staff had been on the ball. I told him I was sorry, but we would not tolerate drinking in the building. He was pleasant and got up and carried his beer out, came back in and seemed to enjoy the show. In all fairness to the Ocean Township police, their presence was always reassuring. We really wanted a place where anyone could come and feel safe.

The show was great and we all had a good time. Too soon it was over and we were on our way home.

From that point on, it all seems to merge into a kaleidoscope of events. The time flew and only the high points are left now in my memory.

Over the next few months, the music continued to draw a nice crowd and we moved to the Saturday night spot that we wanted. We tore down a large wall and made the main room more than twice the size it had been. Now we would stand the real test: could we fill this big of a room? First, we filled it with the sounds of saws and hammers as a stage took shape, and wood paneling began to cover the walls. This was all donated labor and time. We had work parties with as many as forty-five people.

One night I got a hard time about one old fellow who persisted in bringing in a small flask that he was sometimes seen to take a drink from. The musicians who were complaining wanted to know what I was going to do about it. The old man had been a regular at the Homeplace and I had put off saying anything out of respect. Now I was being called to task for it. I went over to him and sat down, and we had a little chat. I told him I was getting my chops busted over his jug and he would have to leave it outside.

"Who is giving you a hard time?" he asked.

I told him who and he laughed. "Merce, you are going to hurt the show if you don't let up on the prohibition around here."

I laughed and told him I was sure that it had reduced the attendance a lot already, but we had a nice group of folks coming in and we could keep it clean and still build Albert Hall.

"Look," I told him, "the only reason I am sitting here right now is because they can see that you have a jug. Put it in a soda can or a Thermos and you won't have any trouble. What they can't see they can't complain about."

It was a cold room that winter and many folks did have a small Thermos that they carried and it worked just fine. The old fellow used to slip me a little of his "coffee" on Saturday night sometimes. It helped.

From that point on our official stance was no drinking. I advised all who asked, however, that we would not be sniffing or tasting people's Thermos bottles or container drinks.

New musicians were coming out of the woodwork. "How do you get to play here?" they would ask. I would then proceed to tell them what we were about and what we were trying to do. If they wanted to play, I needed to hear them do a couple of songs and if they were any good at all, they could have a twenty-minute set. The audience was kind and encouraging to new musicians, and I was to watch some young people become excellent.

There were some who came to me and said they would like to play but only had a tune or two. For them we generally used a part of the intermission time and they would play while the folks waited for the main show to begin.

I was also having problems with a small but vocal minority who felt the show should revolve around them. They felt they should play all evening while the rest of the musicians joined them for a song or two.

The group that had wanted $500 to play was now playing for the small pay we provided.

Not only that, they had to leave early to play their bar gig and they did not like that much either. If they did not play with us, they would lose face with those who supported the project, and in their eyes I had caused the whole problem. One of them told me flat out one night, "We want to see the project fail."

You need a few lemons to make lemonade and I did have some lemons. I tried not to let that faze me and went right on pushing the project.

Early on, Arlene and I went to the bank with two musicians and opened an account that we called the Albert Hall Building Fund. Since they were prominent among their peers I asked if they would secure the account with their Social Security number. I owed the Internal Revenue Service a small amount of money and I did not want to risk them coming in and raiding the account, as I knew they sometimes did. The other signers declined and the account was opened with my Social Security number.

Arlene and I read everything we could get our hands on that applied to crowd control, production, and what we were doing with the music. We were concerned with the size of the crowds and wanted to avoid trouble if at all possible.

I was sitting talking to Joe Albert one night when one of the staff came up and asked if they could do some small job. I told them, "Sure, go ahead and do it." They were happy and went off to do whatever it was.

Joe laughed at the enthusiasm on the youngster's face. He turned to me and said, "Give them the job that wants it, eh, Merce?"

"That's good advice," I told him, and from then on it got to be one of my favorite sayings.

It was a cold winter playing music in the poorly heated and uninsulated auction building, but we hung on and as spring came, so seemed to come new life to the music. I had called the show, "The Sounds of the Jersey Pines." The name is an obvious takeoff on *The Sound of Music.* I hoped the public would draw the unconscious connection.

▲　▲　▲

I became more and more worried about the building fund carrying my Social Security number and also about getting the whole project incorporated. I started approaching individuals whom I thought would make good candidates for the first board of directors, and some accepted. I had promised that we would incorporate in some fashion. I was not more specific, because I was not sure how to do it myself.

About three-and-a-half months into the project I was approached by one of the musicians. They wanted to have a meeting at Joe Albert's about alcohol. They were from the vocal minority, but I agreed to attend. We had almost no problems and it was much ado about nothing, I felt. But since it was at the Homeplace and I liked to visit Joe Albert, I agreed to go.

When the meeting got underway, I was shocked. The meeting was not about drinking. What they wanted me to do was take the music show as a private business and let them have the Albert Hall Building Fund. They wanted to form a nonprofit group to administer the fund. This was an audacious and unacceptable idea and I wanted no part of it.

As I can remember, there were only Arlene and myself and the two musicians who were present, who were a part of the first show and knew the terms I had set up with the rest of the musicians. We were ambushed big-time. I thought about walking out.

I looked over at Joe Albert and I could see he was upset. He knew it was an ambush, too. I remembered him saying, "Give them the job that wants it, eh, Merce?" What was even stranger, I could hear Joe Reid in my head and I remembered his advice to me when we were starting the Baymen's Association. He said, "All you have to do is have a meeting and declare yourself to be a nonprofit corporation and you can begin to operate as one. You must begin to work on the charter and other legal work, but you can start to operate." He also told me at that time to acquire a *Robert's Rules of Order* and study parliamentary procedure.

I was startled to remember Joe's words. Here, coming into my mind, was the information I needed on how to incorporate. Why I could not access it before I do not know.

I left no doubt in anyone's mind that the show and the building fund must go hand-in-hand — one is for the other. They will not be separated. I had no objection to forming a nonprofit corporation to administer the music and the show, as long as the rules were followed and there were open elections.

This for me was a solution to some of my biggest worries, among them the building fund with my Social Security number on it. If the IRS attacked the fund, it would cause a scandal and would do major damage to the project. We were collecting a gate and paying the rent, musicians and other expenses as if we were nonprofit. I did not want to become responsible for the taxes.

I was then asked if I would surrender any claim to private ownership of the show if it were to fall under the auspices of a nonprofit corporation. I replied that I would, provided the rules were followed and there were open elections. We voted to do that, and the Pinelands Cultural Society was formed.

I had a bunch of explaining to do, as at least some of the musicians felt I had joined the radical minority. I told them that was not the case. We needed to incorporate and this was the way it was working out. We would hold elections and the best way to make sure that their fears did not come to pass was to join up and vote.

An organizational meeting was set for April 20, 1975, and elections were held. I became the first president and Arlene was elected corresponding secretary, taking care of communications, including the newsletter.

I do not recall that things got any easier in the year that followed. In my memory it is kind of dreamlike, and I remember only the things that made an impact on me.

Joe Albert came up to Arlene and me one night. "I hope you guys aren't mad at me," he said, referring to the ambush.

"No, Joe, we love you and would never get mad at you. This is just fine and we are glad to have the weight off our shoulders; we understand what happened," we told him.

One night a couple of the musicians I liked and trusted came to me and said, "Merce, do you know that so-and-so is saying you almost killed them with your garvey?"

"What are you talking about?" I asked, startled.

"They are saying that you almost ran them down while they were fishing after dark."

My heart sank, and then I remember that I don't go out after dark anymore. I had started taking this precaution because of my involvement with the politics of the bay. I did not want to be accused of anything, and to remain above suspicion was my intent.

I walked about until I found my accuser standing in a small knot of people down by the refreshment stand.

"What are you saying about me now?" I asked. The person looked at me and to my face declared that I had nearly killed them on the bay after dark.

I replied, "I tie my boat between two occupied houses at the end of the street. I have a high-compression 327 Chevy motor with dry stacks and no mufflers. It sounds like a stock car when I start it up. They can hear me up and down the creek. I can't get out the creek without everyone knowing. My boat has not been out after dark in nearly three years. You are mistaken; it was someone else."

The accuser was taken aback, it was easy to see, but I still got a feeble, "It was you; I know your boat."

"You are wrong and I can prove it," I said, and turned and walked away.

True or not, things of this nature do damage to your credibility and to your conscience. Along with that, the possibility of a serious criminal charge exists. If I have any advice to those who would assume a leadership role, it would be, cover your butt. You may get shot at from a direction you don't expect.

I now had some of the vocal minority on my executive board. They were unruly and were causing dissension. I followed Joe Reid's advice and got hold of *Robert's Rules of Order* and enforced parliamentary procedure to maintain order and direction.

▲ ▲ ▲

During my year as the first president of PCS, many wonderful things happened. One major highlight was hosting Pete Seeger as a guest.

One of his friends, Bill Wurst, had come up to me one night at the show. He introduced himself and his wife Joy, and said that Pete might come and play for Albert Hall if we were interested. Of course we were, and I set up a meeting of the board to meet with Bill and plan the appearance.

The meeting went well, and we received a contract with a list of conditions, none of which were unreasonable, and the show was on. He was very generous and it was a benefit for the building fund, as I recall.

We did not have time to showcase all the musicians for twenty minutes, so I came up with the idea of doing a lineup where we each did one song. This would allow us to show a cross-section of the talent base and all could say they had played in the same show with Pete.

A huge throng gathered to see and hear Pete. The hall was filled to capacity and beyond. All along the walls and in any open space before the stage, people waited for the show to begin. I had all the doors opened, including the two outside doors, and the portals were quickly filled by the overflow of the crowd. Somehow, everyone who wanted got to see and hear Pete that night, as far as I know.

Pete did a wonderful show. I never before or after heard the audience sing as they did for Pete Seeger that night. We didn't get to talk to him much, and I don't know what he thought of us as a group. I hope he remembers Albert Hall and returns to play again some day.

During this time, the show and the society continued to grow, with more and more musicians coming to play. According to the paperwork on hand, in the first six months 190 musicians performed. They and all of the numerous staff members worked for the fun and the concept of sharing the music.

▲   ▲   ▲

As election time approached, I decided it was time for someone else to take over the reins. If the project were to survive, it needed to be able to do it without me. I could only hope that we had endowed the project with enough form and solidity to make it difficult for my successor to alter or change the basic concept of what we were trying to do.

For a year and a half now, my music had been on the back burner. I used my music to fill in wherever it was needed — to start the show, to fill in for a no-show — sometimes I did not get to play at all. Saturday night was one big managerial session and I really just wanted to play music.

Again, some people felt that I was letting them down, and all kinds of dire prophecies were forecast. I stuck to my guns and told them to vote for the best candidate or run for the post themselves. I told them that I would be on the board for a year by virtue of my past presidency and would do what I could to keep an eye on things.

Elections were held and I did just that, although I found the new board quite hard to work with. The building had a small room over the stage that we used as an office. It had no ventilation and was very hot in the summer. We felt that the records were important documents and I was very worried that fire or some other disaster would cause them to be lost. I asked Angus Gillespie, director of the New Jersey Folklore Archive, if he would be interested in placing them in the archives at Rutgers University, and he agreed. That being the case, all the records from the first show to the last show over which I presided are in the archives at Rutgers.

Although Arlene and I did try to work with the society, we wound up doing less and less. Part of the reason is found in music. We were playing out a lot and for the next few years were very busy.

To make a long story short, I formed a new group and with the permission of the original Pinehawkers, re-used the name. We played for groups, schools, colleges, and the state folk festival. We played for the state Council on the Arts many times, governors conventions, and on the boardwalk in Atlantic City. I played on 42nd Street in New York, and at the Smithsonian Institution's Festival of American Folklife in Washington DC in 1983.

Along with the tape of my father's music, I also made a tape of my own music for Marimac Recordings and included guest artists. We also performed on soundtracks for video productions for several clients. Much of this work came from the excellent publicity we received from Arlene's diligent work in that field.

By 1983 the phone was ringing to call us back to PCS. People were coming by the house telling me, "You have to do something; they are killing it." Among the many complaints were of financial misdoing. Some of those bringing the message claimed to be eyewitnesses. I was asked to run for president and to see what I could do to get the project back on track. It was the last thing either Arlene or I wanted, but we were deeply concerned, and so I ran and was elected president in the tenth year of the project.

One of the first things I did was to set up a system whereby two executives would pick up the proceeds from the various departments. They would witness and sign for the monies, and then the cash would be carried to a night deposit box after the show.

I forced the treasurer to at least show paperwork indicating the funds were where they were supposed to be. I wanted an independent auditor but the board was satisfied that all was in order, and I let the matter rest.

I also put out the smoking lamp in Albert Hall, and we were smoke-free.

It was a successful year with increases in all areas. But as it drew to a close I was having some big problems with my health. Each Saturday night would find me with chest pain and I knew I should not be exposing myself to the stress involved in managing the project. Again, I made it known that I would not run for re-election. I had been hoping I would be able to work with the new board, but that was not to be the case.

Arlene and I withdrew from the project, and, except for playing now and then at the hall, have remained remote. In November of '99, we visited the new Albert Hall. The hall is beautiful, the sound is great, and the people were wonderful to us. They gave us a lovely plaque to hang on our wall and we were pleased. I do hope as time goes by that PCS will continue the basic concept we learned at the Homeplace, where all were welcome and all got to play if they wanted to.

Epilogue

Merce and Arlene at their home in Shirley, West Virginia.

I did not want to leave the bay and the lifestyle that I had followed for most of my life. I worked awhile for the Barnegat Bay Research Project. One of the things I did was to put a one-quarter-inch wire mesh on one of my rakes and take a biologist about the bay looking for seed clams. We found that there were almost none to be caught, although we looked at several sites.

I had wanted to do this for years. It was common knowledge that it was against the law to catch seed clams, and I was reluctant to break the law. After the project was over, I left the wire on the rake and went on looking for seed clams up and down our bays. I was disappointed to find the results were the same wherever I went. There were no seed clams or very few. I knew that there were some tough times coming for the baymen. Even if the following season were to bring exceptional recruitment, it would be some years until the new stocks were big enough to be harvested.

Along with declining stocks, health problems were taking their toll on me. I could not work the long day that I was used to. Meanwhile, the cost of living on the Jersey shore was climbing out of sight. Our taxes on our property were more than my original mortgage had been when we bought our small house.

It was easy to see that there would be no laid-back retirement for me. I began to feel that this was not the place to spend my declining years. Arlene and I talked about it and decided to sell our house and try to make a new life for ourselves in some other place.

I was thinking about Tennessee; I had some good friends from the service down there. We got in our car and headed out. We decided to stop in and visit our daughter Ginny and our grandson Justin, who lived in West Virginia. We were so impressed by the people there and the land, that we never made it to Tennessee. We looked at an old farmhouse that was secluded in a "holler," and we loved it. We stayed a few days and went on back to New Jersey.

It would take us another year to sell our home and move out to West Virginia. I went to real estate school and got my license. Along with that, I had basic carpentry skills and I thought I could make a modest living for us. The land is bountiful, with plenty of game and I knew I would never starve as long as the land would feed me. The people are of English and Indian extraction and I found the culture to be much the same as in the pines and shore area that we had come from.

We bought a used Cadillac — if I were going to sell real estate I would need a good car — and we headed for West Virginia. Here, I go on playing music and writing about the land. It is much similar to the life I knew in my youth.

I was honored to have October 14, 1995 named as Merce Ridgway Day in Ocean County by the Board of Freeholders and to receive the Hurley Conklin Award at the Old-Time Barnegat Bay Decoy and Gunning Show the following year.

I will never lose my love of the waters that I was raised on, and I often consider that I have two homes now. One is by the shore; the other is in the West Virginia hills.

Acknowledgements

I would like to extend my sincere thanks to all who encouraged me in this project. This would include Ray Fisk, my publisher; Maria Scandale, editor; and cousin Pooch Buchholz. Also, my cousins Russ Horner and Phil Grant, as well as Chief Listens-to-Whippoorwill. I would thank my great-grandfather Joel Haywood Ridgway, who was the second Captain of the Barnegat Life Saving Station but the first to keep records. He taught me the importance of writing it all down.

My family, who encouraged me to go on, from my Mom and sisters to our daughters and our son, Tom, I thank you all.

I owe the biggest thank you to my dear wife Arlene, who insisted from the start that it was a story worth writing. She persisted when I would have forgotten all about it, and without a doubt, without her it would not exist. Thank you, Dear.

▲ ▲ ▲

One of the many purposes of this book is to be able to clear up some of the mist which has obscured the origins of the "Sounds of the Jersey Pines" and the Albert Hall project. At the same time I would like to make a part of history the pivotal roles that some people played. Those people and their contributions were:

Dave Rinear — Early discussion of project.

Phil Grant — Early discussion of the project and advanced project discussion.

Pete Curry — Coined the name 'Albert Hall'.

Mrs. Howard — Took my arm and led me off to talk to her husband. Had she not done that, there would not have been a first show.

Arlene Ridgway — When I balked, she said the words, "If you don't do it now it will never get done." Had she not said that, there would not have been a first show in the auction building.

The following is a list of the people with whom I personally dialogued or discussed the first show and the creation of a nonprofit entity in the three weeks prior to the first event. Many were musicians and some were staff. They were: Bill Britton, Rick Cortez, Pete Curry, Kathy DeAngelo, Fred Denice, Gladys Eayre, Cathy Foreman, Jon Foreman, Carol Blouch Gille, Robert Gille, Virginia Gille, Wendy Gille, Phil Grant, Kim Hammersma, Karl Hazelwood, Barbara Herr, Russ Herr, Joe Horner, Russ Horner, Scotty Howard, Mrs. Howard, Dennie Jensen, Debra Lofrano, Lewis London, Mark Lynch, Chill Paul, Gerry Pawliski, Skipper Pike, Arlene Ridgway, Dave Ridgway, Joe Rizzo, Max Suckling, John Rose, Janice Sherwood.

The following folks either worked or played music for the first show. Some, as in the case of Joe Albert, just wanted to play music and were not interested in the politics: Joe Albert, Randy Bailey, Chris Byrne, Steve Byrne, Fred Cable, Doug Hand, Sam Hunt, Kurt Kievel, Joe King, Chuck Paul, Mary Ann Paul, John Peich, Pat Von Schmidt, Myrtle Willburn.

These were the folks who made the first show possible and they all share the position of being the founding fathers and mothers of the Albert Hall project. Together, including myself, we are forty-eight in number.

Photograph Credits

All uncredited photographs are from the collection of the author. Photographs credited below are either provided by the photographer or from the author's collection and may be protected by separate copyright: page 150 — Donna Allman; page 39 — Marc Bellagamba/ *The SandPaper;* pages 12, 55, 143 — Ray Fisk; pages 44, 64, 65, 127 — Russ Horner; page 215 — Maria Scandale; pages 1, 134 — N.J. Division of Shellfisheries.

Index

Down The Shore Publishing specializes in books, calendars, cards and videos about New Jersey and the Shore. For a free catalog of all our titles or to be included on our mailing list, just send us a request:

Down The Shore Publishing
P.O. Box 100
West Creek, NJ 08092

www.down-the-shore.com